POWERFUL IMAGES

JAMES EARLE FRASER (1876–1953)

End of the Trail (1918)

Bronze; height 33¾ × base width 6½ × base length 20¾ in.

Buffalo Bill Historical Center, Clara Peck Purchase Fund (112.67)

Fraser's silhouette of a dejected Indian on his dispirited horse is one of the most often-repeated images of an Indian subject. The monumental version of this sculpture, placed in California for the Panama-Pacific International Exposition, symbolized the common belief that the Indian race faced extinction. The pathos of the image implied that this was sad, but inevitable. The sculpture is, however, open to many interpretations. With the persistence of Indian peoples, it has also become an emblem for the passing of a particular way of life, the nomadic life of the Plains.

POWERFUL IMAGES

Portrayals of Native America

SARAH E. BOEHME

GERALD T. CONATY

CLIFFORD CRANE BEAR

EMMA I. HANSEN

MIKE LESLIE

JAMES H. NOTTAGE

FOREWORD BY PETER HASSRICK

INTRODUCTION BY DAVE WARREN

Published by Museums West

in association with the University of Washington Press

Seattle & London

Copyright © 1998 by Museums West

Designed by Audrey Meyer

Printed in Singapore

FIRST EDITION

05 04 03 02 01 03 02 01 00 99

Library of Congress Cataloging-in-Publication Data

Powerful images : portrayals of Native America / Sarah E. Boehme . . . [et al.] ; foreword by Peter Hassrick ; introduction by David Warren.

    p.   cm.

   Includes bibliographical references and index.

    ISBN 0-295-97675-6 (paper: alk. paper)   ISBN 0-295-97697-7 (cloth: alk. paper)

1. Indian art—North America—Exhibitions.   2. Indians in art—North America—Exhibitions.

3. Indians in popular culture—North America—Exhibitions.   I. Boehme, Sarah E.

E98.A7P68   1998

704.9′4997000497—dc21   97-40098

                                                CIP

ILLUSTRATION PAGE VIII

Lakota feather bonnet with trailer, South Dakota (ca. 1890)
Eagle feathers, buckskin, glass beads, tin cones, porcupine quills,
otter and ermine skins, horse hair, ribbon, pigments; 90 × 48 in.
Buffalo Bill Historical Center, Katherine Bradford McClellan Collection,
Gift of The Coe Foundation

Among Northern Plains tribes, eagle feather war bonnets were reserved for men of high status as symbols of their leadership and skills as warriors. Over time, the war bonnet assumed new meanings both within and outside of native communities. For many people, the timeless image of the Plains warrior on horseback in his flowing feather war bonnet, as photographed by Edward Curtis and portrayed in novels, Wild West shows, and film, has come to represent all Indian people and the American West.

Santa Domingo olla, New Mexico (ca. 1900)

H 14¼ in., D 17⅛ in.

Eiteljorg Museum of American Indians and Western Art

MUSEUMS WEST

Amon Carter Museum   *Fort Worth, Texas*

Autry Museum of Western Heritage   *Los Angeles, California*

Buffalo Bill Historical Center   *Cody, Wyoming*

Eiteljorg Museum of American Indians and Western Art   *Indianapolis, Indiana*

Gilcrease Museum   *Tulsa, Oklahoma*

Glenbow Museum   *Calgary, Alberta, Canada*

The Heard Museum   *Phoenix, Arizona*

National Cowboy Hall of Fame   *Oklahoma City, Oklahoma*

The National Museum of Wildlife Art   *Jackson, Wyoming*

Rockwell Museum   *Corning, New York*

Contents

Foreword

PETER HASSRICK

*L*IKE EVERYONE ELSE, AMERICAN INDIANS OWN ONLY PART OF THEIR PER-
sonal and historical identity. Every individual is a combination of corporeal and spiritual self,
as well as an amalgam of perceptions imposed by the outside world. We all like to believe that
we are truly ourselves, that what others think of us is not central to our being, but in truth
those external conceptions, whether observations or expectations, ultimately influence who
we really are.

The inescapable nature of this varies only by degree. When the external force is particularly strong, be it the family or parent of the individual or a dominant culture for a group of
people, it is sometimes more difficult for the individual or group to hold onto the corporeal/
spiritual essence. Native Americans especially have suffered from this phenomenon.

Artists and writers, anthropologists and politicians, have over centuries enshrouded their
impressions upon America's native peoples, shaping through their images, their analyses,
their prejudices and motivations the public perception of who the Indian is and how to
know, appreciate, and, too often, manipulate Indian culture. Despite the diversity of native
North American cultures, languages, economies and individuals, images in the popular
imagination have tended to be generalized and one-dimensional. Analysis of these generalized images reveals that their roots are based on many of the depictions of artists and writers
of the nineteenth century. The images have been repeated, layer upon layer, in political, historical and commercial contexts, with a resultant blurring of perceptions of contemporary
Native American people in the public imagination.

From the earliest years of this nation's existence, museums have also played a vital role in
establishing and perpetuating public perceptions of native life. The first proposed national
museums were not displays of pilgrim curiosities, but collections of portraits of leading
Indian figures as limned by George Catlin or Charles Bird King. The Peale Museum, while
proudly presenting likenesses of the nation's founding fathers next to specimens of natural
science, exposed and interpreted Indian objects and scenes from Indian life collected at the
foot of the Rockies as early as 1819.

In America's museums, these most public of venues, native peoples have been variously held up as aboriginal curiosities, romantic *beaux idéals*, vestiges of disappearing innocence, resisters of Anglo megalomania, artistically creative masters, Rousseauian children of nature, the "true" Americans, and models of quaintly amusing exotica. Over the years, the popular images of Native Americans have also become increasingly regionalized, symbolic now of the American West. As powerful cultural icons, they have been propagated through art, literature, museums, film and advertising.

In 1990, a group of museums came together as the consortium Museums West. They defined themselves as "an international group of collegial institutions organized for the purpose of developing and expanding an awareness and an appreciation of the North American West." Together, they searched for a meaningful, cooperative project to which they could lend their mutual efforts and share their collections, staff input and audiences. They chose to organize a joint exhibition, one which would contribute to public understanding about some broad segment of their collective holdings. This exhibition, *Powerful Images*, is the culmination of that collaboration.

The organizing principle of this book and the accompanying exhibition is, in itself, an analysis of perceptions and what has governed their creation, drawing on views of Indian people both from within and from outside native cultures. The Indian voice and perspective is far more varied and complex than that of the Anglo, which tends to be relatively monolithic and entrenched. In both cases, this project invites a better understanding of American and Canadian societies by examining the symbolism related to images of Native Americans which are prevalent in North American cultures. It is further intended to encourage a public audience to examine their own perceptions of Native Americans, to begin to understand how those perceptions have been formed and become generalized over time. The project also endeavors to provide insight into the creation of history and how North American culture has understood itself at critical moments in the past. And, finally, it is hoped that, as a result of this investigation and presentation, the American public might enjoy a better understanding of the importance of Indian images of North American cultural history.

Introduction

DAVE WARREN

What soon became known as the "New World" was in fact the old world, the oldest world we know, the world the West had once been. Now the onward press of Christian history brought a civilization into contact with its psychic and spiritual past, and this was a contact for which it was utterly unprepared. The ensuing conflict was so deep that it has yet to be resolved or even understood.[1]

*P*OWERFUL IMAGES: PORTRAYALS OF NATIVE AMERICA REFLECTS THE "Mythic Zone"[2] that Frederick Jackson Turner described in the contact of Western Europeans and the native people in a new land. It was, and metaphorically continues to be, a place of uncertainty for the newly arrived, but for the native peoples of the land, it is a region clearly marked, where natural world and spiritual life ways commingle, explaining the continuum of origin and destiny.

The Mythic Zone was "out there," beyond the line of settlement and some familiar boundary of intellectual terrain. The metaphors abound. Just as European plowshares imprinted the soil, signifying possession of space, control over the very nature of the land through predictable cultivation, so were efforts made to control, change and dominate the peoples of that place "beyond geography."

So it is that representations of others become part of a process in which one tries to reconcile the unfamiliar with ideals and values we know and accept as a norm. Everything else becomes anomalous, exotic or fearsome. What we sometimes overlook is that the image of others can be caricatured to the point of creating a new reality that does not, or never did, exist. Again, this is the Mythic Zone into which we pile unending meaning.

The essays that accompany *Powerful Images: Portrayals of Native America* are the collective voice of Native Americans who increasingly voice frustration, attempt to educate and explain the meaning of "art" in a larger, more profound context of unprecedented change in their communities. The significance of these writings can be overlooked if one does not fully appreciate the existence of world views and the determining force in contemporary Native America, which is truly undergoing an unprecedented community building process. This process creates conflict with those who cannot reconcile earlier perceptions of native history and culture with the new emergence. Or, as James Clifford describes it,

Something . . . occurs whenever marginal peoples come into a historical or ethnographic space that has been defined by the West's imagination. "Emerging in the modern world," their distinct histories quickly vanish. Swept up in a destiny dominated by the capitalist West and by various technologically advanced socialisms, these suddenly "backward" peoples no longer invent local futures. What is different about them remains tied to traditional pasts, inherited structures that either resist or yield to the new but cannot produce it.[3]

But the futures are being created, as these essays attest. They bear out the insights of those whose writings on cultural contact reveal the complex nature of arts in, and as a function of, culture. Each essay comments on a particular aspect of these facts. Whose judgment prevails in the description of culture? What are the contexts of individual expression in the larger frameworks of constantly shifting social, political, scientific and ideological movements? All these legacies and layers constitute contemporary Native American experience.

These authors also reflect the difficulty of understanding a dynamic that forms the views of people of different cultures. Sarah E. Boehme discusses the forces and factors that led to the formation of the first, and mostly lasting, views of Native American life and people in the nineteenth century. What George Catlin, Seth Eastman and others created were the still life images of American Indians that became gallery shows. Their work became harbingers of the way in which museum collections ultimately interpreted native culture: as people of limited dimension, frozen in space and time. Other artists carried the tradition of such imagery into the next century, continuing or enforcing the hallmark of externally imposed authenticity by limiting images to some notion of what constituted the "authentic past" in racial features and other rigid classifications of what was *real* Indian culture.

Popular art, James Nottage reminds us, also creates cultural images. Perhaps even more than the Catlins, and clearly complementing the mass public impressions of movies, the omnipresence of cigar store Indians, Big Chief writing tablets, and plethora of logos of exaggerated Roman-nosed Braves and football Redskins has commercialized the stereotype, all at the expense of a people. Such "art" reaches everyone, and carries more telling messages, perhaps, than the gallery or museum presentation.

The essays by Gerald Conaty, Clifford Crane Bear and Mike Leslie review the current stage of the "local futures" in Native American art. They are also the messengers, like many other artists in the native community, who describe an emerging Native American nationalism. Such is the commentary of Leslie, who calls for more sensitivity to the particular circumstances that led to the creation of art work in the past. Are the Fort Marion prisoners' ledger drawings less traditional than their contemporaries, whose tipi paintings recount events of other places, farther removed from Florida prison life, but nonetheless experienced by kinsmen of the same tribe at the same time?

It is not surprising that we should find such diversity in the essays for this exhibit. They are commentaries on the changes taking place in Indian society. The public is now more aware of Native Americans. Issues of self-determination—political, economic and cultural—

all form a new environment of change and circumstance. All changes dramatically challenge the old images and notions of Native American passivity and marginality. But most of all, the changes require that any interpretation of Indian art be carefully evaluated in the context of Native Americans in the new paradigm of national life. This trend can be measured on every level of life, including global movements, among all indigenous peoples.[4]

These developments clearly require new approaches to understanding Native Americans, in any areas of cultural expression. In revisionist studies of American Southwest borderlands history, one author suggested the analogy of cubism as one means of incorporating the many dimensions of culture contact and institutional development.[5] Unlike a two-dimensional plane, cubist perspective allows simultaneous and multiple views of the events and issues, in which perspectives can be shifted as the need arises.[6]

Museums and galleries face the same challenge. No longer two-dimensional forums, or the exclusive domain of academics, programs mounted there require a "cubist" perspective to deal with the complexity of the American Indian in our lives. Conaty and Crane Bear write about these dimensions—the people and their connections to special places, the enshrining force of land and place for family, religion, tribe. World views are no more sharply contrasted than in their account of the Cree language, in which certain concepts or terms cannot be translated, or for which no counterpart exists in English. This is no mystery— it is simply another manifestation of the view of worlds that others must accept as reality. But it is just this perception that Native Americans now bring onto canvas, in sculptured stone, the written word, or the moving image of film and video or computer graphics.

Historical truth has always been difficult to come by. And the agenda of the new century will present even greater challenges to those dealing with community. The implications inherent to the redefinition of culture in the local and national life are highly complicated. We, in the United States, are unaccustomed to studying, much less living, ethnicity. Patrick Moynihan, who predicted the breakup of the Soviet Union along its ethnic fault lines, observed nearly a generation ago:

Religion and race define the next state in the evolution of the American peoples. But the American nationality is still forming: Its processes are mysterious, and the final form, if there is ever to be a final form, is as yet unknown.[7]

For Native Americans, art becomes one of the most striking features of the change in national life. It is a different time, not only in the tenor of social change; the shift from institutional instruction of Indian art to individual studios describes an increasingly common highly personalized, self-reliant creativity of all Native American works. Painters, novelists, poets, sculptors, movie and video makers abound, and no longer are exclusively the graduates of institutions that produced the Kiowa Five, or the generation of the Santa Fe Studio or Institute of American Indian Arts, or even earlier, the ledger drawings of men at Fort Marion and students who sat in art classes at the Hampton Institute and Carlisle Indian School. Those places molded the styles, even in their most generous allowance for individualization, of Indian arts. All are critical to the contemporary development of cultural arts in this country and should be recognized as the foundation and points of departure for the profusion of Indian arts that signal contemporary art and cultural landscape.

Emma Hansen considers Indian art and aesthetics as outgrowths of such developments. Underlying them are persistent questions of boundaries—where art ends and ethnographic artifact begins. The issues are epistemological: what purpose does an object serve within its cultural system? How is that object interpreted if there is no term for "art." Rather, we need to understand that the production of what one might call art is integral to a cultural system. From this idea arises the oft-stated observation that indigenous systems consider art a process of "becoming," allowing the essence and form that resides in the clay, ivory or wood reveal itself. "Artists, then, are facilitators, guided by universal orderings. In some ways that inherent nature of Indian art still remains, no matter how modern the piece or contemporary the circumstances that surround its making.

The essays collectively describe the longstanding conflict found in all study and interpretation of native people. It is a question of authority and authentication. Until recently, Western norms have prevailed in determining the answers to these questions. Once dominant, Western visions are now challenged by the experience of the people of traditional culture.

That conflict characterizes revisionist studies. It is the substance of a new history under construction, characterized by a public awareness of *culture*, the means by which we give meaning to the world, and the force that defines self and community—a total and essential function of life.

Museums are at the nexus of this change. They deal with the perplexities of historical perspective and contemporary interpretations, scholarship and the experiences of those who come to their programs. *Historical identity* and *cultural identity* are active agents in the process of understanding culture in human relations.[8] Each brings its own perspectives to the questions of culture and history, continuity and change, and world views.

Historical identity is bound up with a description of events, causes and results, often in linear chronological terms. It is limited, involving immediate interests, closely bound to political and economic systems and ideas. The analysis of human events occurs within disciplines of knowledge—economics, history, even art. Historical identity subtly drives the rationale behind most museum presentations.

Cultural identity derives from the individual's relation to larger, uniquely kindred personal affiliations and a longer view of self in time and place. It depends on solidarity, traditions, ways of living, common religion, all amounting to an internal viewpoint of culture that defines events, institutions, and influences. It is this identity that persists, transcending time and place.

Culture, amorphous as it may be, is a force and factor fully recognized and stressed: what makes people who they are, how they came to be and the explanation of self in complex systems of cultural organizations.

Historical identity of societies and people offers a way to understand the conflicts within societies as well as between peoples and nations torn by multiple historical and cultural allegiances. At the same time, cultural identity is essential to understanding the force that shapes people; it explains ideals and behaviors that historical documents and someone else's logic cannot define. The means of organizing, describing and explaining developments form an eternal set of experiences, through non-native systems, including language and concepts.

Powerful Images: Portrayals of Native America is an exposition of Native American cultural history. We suggest that the opportunity to learn from such exhibitions will increase as more efforts are made to better comprehend the Native American experience. While many techniques are employed in this undertaking, the issues and challenges of interpretations remain as constants. This is simply a reflection of the transition we are entering, and a commentary on the "Mythic Zone," where it all began. For the viewer at such presentations, the full dimension of art in Native American culture can be finally accepted.

1. Frederick Jackson Turner, *Beyond Geography: The Western Spirit Against the Wilderness* (New Brunswick, NJ: Rutgers University Press, 1994), p. 95.

2. *Ibid.*, p. 9.

3. James Clifford, *The Predicament of Culture: Twentieth-Century Ethnography, Literature and Art* (Cambridge: Harvard University Press, 1988), p. 9.

4. The Royal Commission on Aboriginal People recently recommended major changes in Native policy to the Canadian government including, "deal[ing] with aboriginal peoples on a nation to nation basis, recognizing and encouraging the emergence of another order of government." "Canada Pressed on Indian Rights: Commission Urges Self-Rule for Tribes," *Washington Post*, November 22, 1996.

5. David Hurst Thomas, "Columbian Consequences: The Spanish Borderlands in Cubist Perspective," *Columbian Consequences: Archaeological and Historical Perspectives on the Spanish Borderlands*, Vol. 1 (Washington, D.C.: Smithsonian Institution Press, 1989), p. 7.

6. *Ibid.*

7. Nathan Glazer and Daniel P. Moynihan, *Beyond the Melting Pot: The Negroes, Puerto Ricans, Jews, Italians and Irish of New York City* (Cambridge, MA: MIT Press, 1970), p. 315, quoted in Daniel Patrick Moynihan, *Pandaemonium: Ethnicity in International Politics* (New York: Oxford University Press, 1993), p. 32.

8. Exhibits at the Smithsonian National Gallery of Art and National Museum of Air and Space have experienced the stress of the transition. *The West as America* exhibition and the proposed exhibition centering on the Enola Gay produced considerable reaction from exponents of America's historical identity in true Turnerian fashion. In the latter case, veterans of World War II (cultural identities) took strenuous exception to the revisionist interpretation that the Air and Space exhibit would have made to the circumstances surrounding the dropping of the atomic bomb. Interestingly, others have described the historical-cultural identity issue alternatively as the conflict between an academic "historical voice" and the participant "commemorative voice" (see Edward T. Linenthal, "Can Museums Achieve a Balance Between Memory and History?" *CRM Bulletin*, no. 4 [1995]).

Crow cradleboard, Montana (ca. 1915)

Wood, buckskin, cotton cloth, glass beads; 41¾ × 11 in.

Buffalo Bill Historical Center, Gift of Mr. and Mrs. Larry Larom

Among native people, the creation of beautiful cradleboards symbolizes the importance of family and children. The image of the Indian baby strapped in the cradleboard is common in popular culture and sometimes relates to the misconception that native women had no important economic or social roles. Recognition that all members of the family, whether men, women, elders, or children, had important duties is lost.

POWERFUL IMAGES

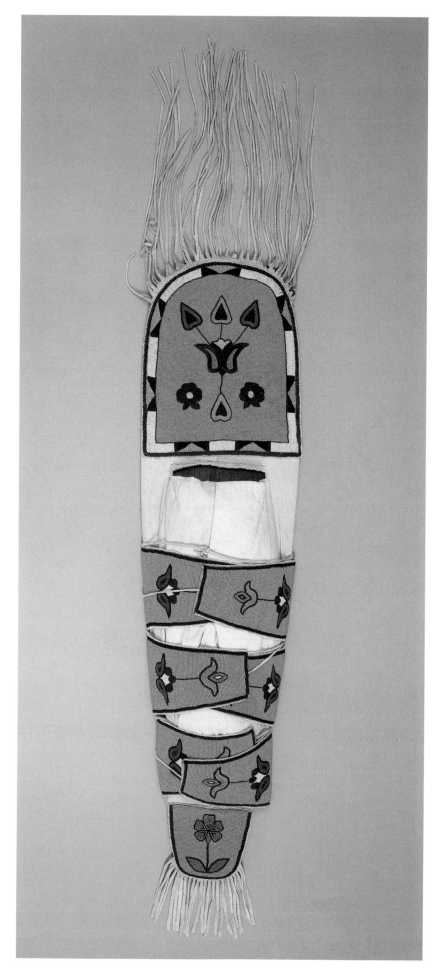

Northern Cheyenne Woman Doing Quillwork,
Lame Deer, Montana (1904)
Buffalo Bill Historical Center, George Bird Grinnell Collection

Powerful Images
Art of the Plains and Southwest

EMMA I. HANSEN

*S*INCE THE FIRST EURO-AMERICAN ARTISTS AND SCIENTISTS OF THE LATE eighteenth and early nineteenth centuries visited native peoples of North America and collected objects representative of their cultures, the traditional arts of American Indian people have been categorized, analyzed and defined by non-native scholars. For the early explorers, including Lewis and Clark, and the artists, George Catlin and Karl Bodmer, their field collections of hide clothing, ornaments, painted hides and other materials were specimens they used to describe and illustrate the Indians they had met.

In the early decades of the twentieth century, many large museum collections were amassed at such institutions as the Field Museum of Natural History by the ethnologist George Dorsey, the Heye Foundation (now the National Museum of the American Indian) by ethnologists employed by George Heye, the Smithsonian Institution by Bureau of American Ethnology researchers, and the American Museum of Natural History by Clark Wissler and others. By then, most of the tribes had been under the control of the reservation system for thirty years or more and the lives of American Indian people had drastically been altered.

The once massive herds of buffalo which had been the centers of the Plains Indians' economic and spiritual lives had been decimated by commercial hide hunters. The people themselves had been reduced by disease, starvation and warfare, some tribes such as the Mandan, Pawnee and Omaha suffering as much as a ninety-five percent population loss by the last half of the nineteenth century.[1] With the loss of lives, homelands and freedom to go beyond the boundaries of the reservations, many people also experienced a loss of spirit and faith in their traditional beliefs and medicines. These conditions allowed for large numbers of objects, which were mistakenly viewed as ethnographic remnants of dying and disappearing cultures, to be purchased by private and museum collectors. Even ceremonial bundles, once the keystones of spiritual life, found their way to museum collections.

Once inside museums, these ethnographic objects were stored, cataloged, preserved and displayed often as natural history specimens of seemingly unchanging nineteenth-century cultures. Lakota anthropologist Bea Medicine describes this process as "laundry

Navajo weavers, Monument Valley

Buffalo Bill Historical Center, Vincent Mercaldo Collection

list anthropology," in which the objects came to define the cultures and "The material goods assumed more dynamic qualities than the people themselves."[2]

Recently, the aesthetic qualities of American Indian art have been emphasized through exhibitions at art museums and galleries. A beautifully carved buffalo horn spoon, collected as an ethnographic specimen in the late nineteenth century, now may be viewed as an example of Plains Indian sculpture and exhibited apart from its tribal context and the artist who created it. Once functional Southwestern pottery is now made for market and prized by collectors for its form and design.

As recent writings have stressed, North American Indian languages have no equivalent word for "art."[3] Traditional Indian materials, while admired within their cultural contexts for craftsmanship or design, were a part of the cultures that produced them and had important economic, social, or spiritual functions. According to Lloyd New:

Although Indians of the past probably never considered themselves to be practicing artists in pursuit of art for its own sake, art was nonetheless integral in the growth of Indian culture. For them, art and culture are inseparable—art is essential to the shaping of culture and simultaneously shaped by it.[4]

Rather than being products of an artistic process, the objects serve as reflections of cultural ideals, beliefs and knowledge. They may manifest the spirituality of a people or support community and individual achievements, aspirations and the proper roles of men and women, children and elders. For the artists, the creative process with its attendant preparations, songs and prayers may have as much value as the completed work. Within the Cheyenne, Arapaho and Lakota tribes, individuals must have the cultural rights to produce certain objects and guilds and societies maintain excellence in skills such as quill work and tipi decorating.[5] A Southern Cheyenne woman described the creation of sacred decorated tipis this way:

These decorated tipis are religious. A woman has to vow to make one. She doesn't just make a beautiful tipi because she wants to. For example, if her baby is sick, she might vow to make a beautiful tipi. Mrs. Black was given the right, from her mother, to mark this kind of a tipi and direct the work. She has a medicine bag with her patterns and marking things and medicines. She names all the women that have owned the bag before her. She invites these women, known tipi makers, and their spirits and prays to them.[6]

Traditional artists consider the gathering of materials such as clay or wood a sacred act and give thanks to the Creator for these gifts. Often prayers and songs such as this Tewa Song of the Sky Loom are offered to guide the creative endeavor:

Oh our Mother the Earth, oh our Father the Sky.
Your children are we, and with tired backs
We bring you the gifts that you love.
Then weave for us a garment of brightness:
May the warp be the white light of morning.
May the weft be the red light of evening.
May the fringes be the falling rain,
May the border be the standing rainbow.
Then weave for us a garment of brightness

That we may walk fittingly where birds sing.
That we may walk fittingly where grass is green,
Oh our Mother the Earth, oh our Father the Sky.[7]

There is incredible diversity in native cultures of North America, evident in their different languages, economies and lifeways. The tribal groups of the Plains and Southwestern regions are probably most familiar. Images of the Lakota or Cheyenne warrior on horseback with his eagle feather war bonnet or the Navajo weaver or Puebloan potter have been repeated time and time again. What more can the traditional art of the Plains and Southwest reveal about the people who created and used these objects?

A Place in the Universe

East of my grandmother's house the sun rises out of the plain. Once in his life a man ought to concentrate his mind upon the remembered earth, I believe. He ought to give himself up to a particular landscape in his experience, to look at it from as many angles as he can, to wonder about it, to dwell upon it. He ought to imagine that he touches it with his hands at every season and listens to the sounds that are made upon it. He ought to imagine the creatures there and all the faintest motions of the wind. He ought to recollect the glare of noon and all the colors of the dawn and dusk.[8]

The Plains and the Southwest present contrasting environments, each with its own challenges to the peoples who live there. The Great Plains comprise a vast region of North America stretching from the Mississippi in the east to the foothills of the Rocky Mountains in the west and from Canada south to Texas. Despite the extremities of the Plains environment—frequent droughts, sudden thunderstorms and variable temperatures—native people found a richness in the tall grass prairies, which supported herds of grazing buffalo, deer, elk and antelope, and in the fertile river valleys, where Mandan, Hidatsa, Pawnee, Omaha and Arikara women tilled gardens of corn, beans and squash.

Although both nomadic hunting and village farming traditions had coexisted on the Plains for hundreds of years, the eighteenth and nineteenth centuries witnessed the dramatic rise of the warrior and hunter tradition. During this period, tribes including the Cheyenne, Arapaho and Lakota acquired horses through Spanish settlements in the Southwest and guns from French and American traders, and moved into the Plains from their original homelands in the Great Lakes, Plateau and Great Basin regions. The material culture of the Plains was based upon mobility. Both farmers and the more nomadic hunters traveled in pursuit of the buffalo at least seasonally, living in portable hide tipis and carrying their belongings with them.

In the arid Southwest of present New Mexico and Arizona, from about A.D. 800 to 1270, the Anasazi, ancestors of later Puebloan groups, lived communally in adobe villages along river valleys where they were able to grow their traditional gardens. For Puebloan peoples, the use of clay in pottery and the development of tribally distinctive ceramics has roots centuries old and continues to tie the people to their traditions and their lands. The Navajo, an Athabascan-speaking people, moved into the region about A.D. 1400, adopting sheepherding from the Spanish and textile weaving from Puebloan groups. Co-existing in the Southwest from the early historical period to the present were Apachean groups and the Pima and Papago located along the Salt and Gila rivers.

Within both Native American and Euro-American cultures, art has served to order and interpret an individual's role within his or her environment and universe as a whole. Among native cultures, religion, which is integral to all aspects of daily lives, helps to answer universal questions. The designs of many objects of traditional art represent a spirituality which acknowledges the power and authority of the Creator and symbolizes the relationship of the people to the earth and sky.

The earth and the sky together represent a whole, with elements of each including plants, animals, rocks, sun moon, earth and people all related, a "single breath," in the words of Laguna poet Leslie Marmon Silko.

> You see the sky now
> colder than the frozen river
> so dense and white
> little birds walk across it.
>
> You see the sky now
> but the earth is lost in it
> and there are no horizons.
> It is all a single breath.
>
> You see the sky but the earth is called
> by the same name
> the moment
> the wind shifts
> sun splits it open
> and bluish membranes
> push through slits of skin.
>
> You see the sky[9]

Throughout the Plains and Southwest, carved or painted images on rock have been found near rivers and streams, along cliff facings and in caves. Petroglyphs were created by pecking or scratching the surface of the rock with a smaller stone. Some of the carvings were painted with natural pigments, while others, known as pictographs, consisted only of painted designs. In the Southwest, the images range from geometric forms to representations of animals and humans hunting, dancing or playing flutes.

In the Big Horn Mountains of Wyoming and Montana and other areas of the Northern Plains region, rock art images consist of abstract marks such as circles, animal tracks and human handprints and footprints, and images of animals, humans such as shield-bearing warriors, and supernatural or spiritual representations. Animals, including buffalo, elk, deer, mountain sheep, bears, and eagles and other birds, seem to predominate and reflect the ritual importance of hunting as an economic activity. Some images with both human forms and animals may be biographical, depicting specific events commemorated by an individual. Supernatural beings, some with horned heads or wings, seem to radiate power.[10]

Although there is little definitive written information on these images, which date from approximately 2500 B.C. through the middle of the 1800s, many continue to be meaningful

EDWARD S. CURTIS (1868–1952), photographer
A Painted Tipi—Assiniboine (1907)
Photogravure; Buffalo Bill Historical Center

**Petroglyphs at Legend Rock in Wyoming with human figures,
hand print, images of big horn sheep, elk and deer**
Photograph by Michael Bies

Rock art near Thermopolis, Wyoming
Photograph by Michael Bies

Supernatural figures predominate in the rock art at this site.

to Indian people, as evidenced by oral traditions, beliefs and practices. In his writings, George Bird Grinnell described a site known as Painted Rocks on the Northern Cheyenne reservation, which the people consider mysterious because the pictures appeared on the rocks "without anyone having painted them." In the early 1900s, Painted Rocks was remembered by Cheyenne warriors as a place to pray for success in battles and to leave offerings.[11]

Among Plains cultures, images of animals can be found beaded or painted on clothing, painted on shields and lodge covers, and carved on quirts and dance sticks. Animal symbolism also appears in body painting. They prevail in oral traditions and stories, and dances and songs, reflecting not only their economic importance, but also their spiritual significance. Among the Pawnee, animals were depicted in dances and dramas organized by societies of men. Membership in these societies came about through visions during which an individual encountered an animal and gained special wisdom from the experience. During the Okipa ceremony recorded by George Catlin and Karl Bodmer, before beginning their winter buffalo hunt, Mandan and Hidatsa men dressed as buffalo and performed dances to bring about successful hunts.[12]

As the largest mammal and essential source of food and materials for clothing, lodge covers, and other necessities, the buffalo was the center of ceremonial life for Plains hunters. Among horticultural Plains tribes, ceremonies devoted to corn, tobacco, and mother earth balance the hunting ceremonies. Other animals depicted in art and the qualities they represent include the grizzly bear, because of its inherent strength and power, the elk and wolf, and eagles and other birds, which are symbols of power and messengers to the heavens.

Specific objects such as the Black Buffalo or Never Sits Down Shield may be associated with their own oral traditions rich in symbolism. According to Siksika tribal member Ben Calf Rope,

Eagle Child was the seventh son of a Siksika. One day young Eagle Child was out looking for horses and saw on the side of a hill a herd of buffalo lying down. It was a hot day and Eagle Child went down to a spring to get a drink of water. After drinking he lay on the ground and went to sleep. He then had a dream. In the dream he saw seven buffalo bulls coming down to the spring. The first bull had a shield around his neck. This buffalo said to Eagle Child, "My boy, go away so that we can drink at the spring for we are very thirsty." He then said, "Here is my shield. You will be strong and brave and all the animals will protect you." He then gave the shield to Eagle Child.

When Eagle Child was about eighteen years old there was a fight between some Crow and the Siksika. The Crow began to run away and Eagle Child, carrying the shield, ran after them. The leader of the Crows on reaching the top of a hill stopped and, facing the Siksika shouted that the boy's name should not be Eagle Child but he should be called "Never Sits Down." He knew that the boy was carrying very powerful medicine. From that time on the shield was known as the "Never Sits Down" shield and was always carried in tribal warfare.[13]

Symbols of the universe, including stars, the full moon and the crescent moon, combined with oral traditions, also helped to define an individual's place in the universe. Pawnee elders studied the constellations and had sophisticated knowledge of the sky's formations, which they depicted in star charts painted on hides. Origin stories from many tribes contain references to the sun and the moon depicted by the spiritual figures, Morning Star and Evening Star, as essential elements.

Blackfoot model tipi, Alberta

Canvas, beads, pigments, wood; H 27 in., D 27 in.; Glenbow Museum

11

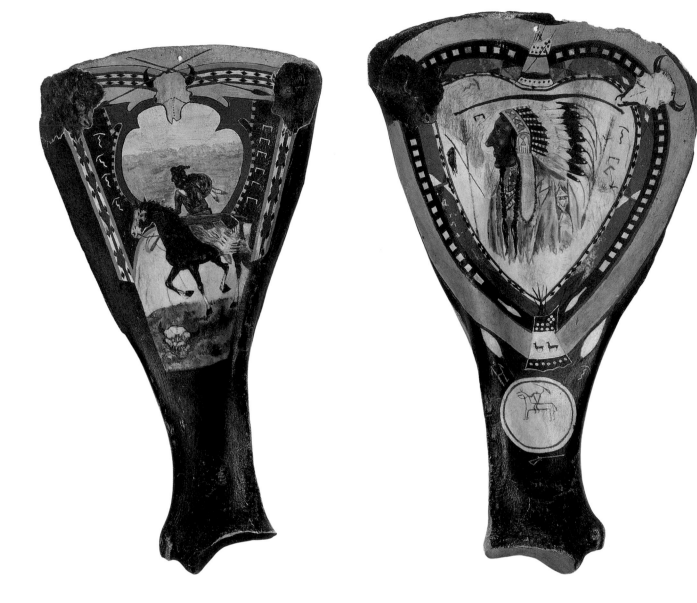

TWO GUN (PERCY PLAINWOMAN)
Paintings on moose scapula, Blood Reserve, Alberta, Canada
14 × 8½ in. and 13 × 7½ in.; Glenbow Museum

Dakota pipe, Northern Plains

Catlinite, wood, beads; 42 × 6 in.; Glenbow Museum

Assiniboine or Gros Ventre feather bonnet, Fort Belknap Reservation, Montana (ca. 1885)
Eagle feathers, wool cloth, ermine and weasel skins, glass beads, horse hair;
17½ × 10¾ in.; Buffalo Bill Historical Center, Chandler-Pohrt Collection,
Gift of Mr. and Mrs. Richard A. Pohrt, Jr.

Plains Indian people consider the eagle to be the most powerful of birds and
its tail feathers arrayed in war bonnets offered protection in battle. Men earned
the right to wear the feathers through courageous deeds and valor.

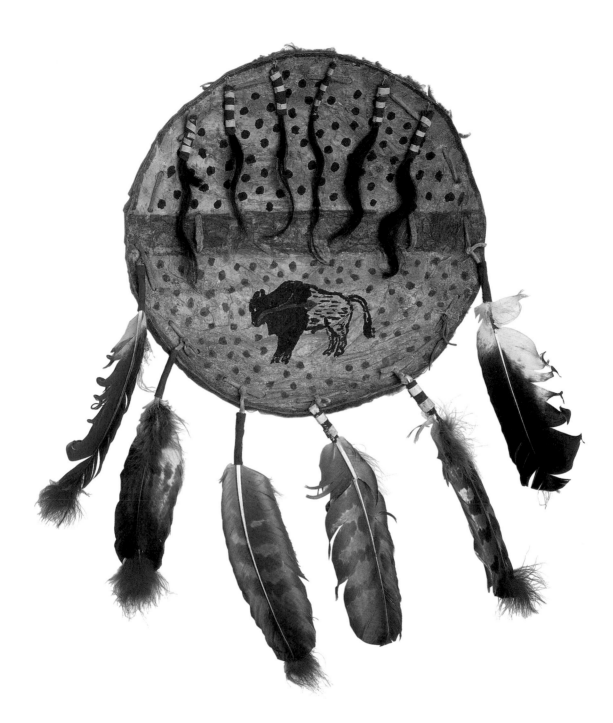

Black Buffalo or Never Sits Down Shield, Siksika, Alberta
Rawhide, eagle feathers, hair, pigments, trade cloth; D 17 in.
Glenbow Museum

Ghost Dance clothing included elements of the earth and the sky and animals with importance in the spirit world—eagles, magpies, crows and turtles, which symbolized longevity. The omniscience of the crow as the messenger from the spirit world is depicted in an Arapaho Ghost Dance song:

> I hear everything,
> I hear everything,
> I am the crow,
> I am the crow.[14]

The Ghost Dance came to Plains tribes under the leadership of the Paiute visionary, Wovoka, in 1889–90. At this time the Plains peoples had reached the nadir of their existence; they had been decimated by disease and starvation on the reservation, and many of their most important traditions were in danger of being lost forever. Wovoka taught that people could bring back their old way of life by performing the Ghost Dance, living peacefully and working hard. The buffalo and other game would once again be plentiful, dead relatives and friends would return, and white men would disappear. An Arapaho Ghost Dance song describes the predicted creation of the new earth:

> My children, my children,
> Look! the earth is about to move,
> Look! the earth is about to move,
> My father tells me so,
> My father tells me so.[15]

Recording History

Art may be used to record and retell cultural and personal histories. Biographical art, as well as depictions of specific historic events, appear in petroglyphs, hide paintings, tipi covers, ledger art and in other forms. For example, historical figures consisting of Spanish armies on horseback were recorded on rock walls in Canyon de Chelly National Monument in Arizona, purportedly by a Navajo artist named Dibe' Yazhi sometime during the early 1800s. The drawings depict Spanish horsemen and Indians who entered the canyon during the winter of 1804–1805 and killed more than one hundred Navajos in what is now known as Massacre Cave.[16]

For Plains Indian people, winter counts on robes or in ledgers commemorate the important events of each year. Pictographic hide paintings, lodge covers and ledger drawings may record a warrior's accomplishments in capturing horses or in battle. Among many Indian people, such war deeds are accredited to assistance from more powerful beings. Retelling the stories and recording them on robes, lodge covers or in ledger art reinforces and reminds the people of those blessings. This tradition carries into contemporary powwows, where war veterans carry the American flag as well as the eagle feathered staff as they lead dancers into the arena during the Grand Entry. During ceremonies, veterans recount their war deeds, once again reinforcing important cultural values and the individual's role in supporting those values.

Objects also may symbolize important biographical events. Images of horses, human heads or other figures carved into wooden dance sticks were carried in Victory Dances by

Dakota painted buffalo hide robe, Northern Plains (ca. 1883)
Buffalo hide, pigments; 82 × 69 in.; Rockwell Museum

Men of the Plains often wrapped themselves in robes made of whole
skins of buffalo painted with pictographic or geometric designs.
Women specialized in painting the geometric images of the feather
bonnet robe with a central figure of the sun and feathers radiating
from it in circles representative of a war bonnet.

17

Siksika man's shirt, Alberta

Buckskin, porcupine quills, hawk bells, feathers, hair, pigments;
35 × 20½ in.; Glenbow Museum

Plains Indian clothing and other objects may contain elements of
the earth and sky. The black dots on the upper half of the shirt are
thought to represent hailstones.

Southern Arapaho Ghost Dance shirt, Oklahoma (ca. 1890)
Elk hide, eagle feathers, pigments; 40 × 24½ in.
Buffalo Bill Historical Center, Chandler-Pohrt Collection,
Gift of The Searle Family Trust and The Paul Stock Foundation

Birds such as eagles, magpies and crows serve as spiritual messengers
to the heavens. The constellations of the sky, the turtle representing
long life and the earth, and the bird spiritual messengers are
important in Ghost Dance symbology.

Hopi Kachina doll, Arizona (ca. 1900)
Wood, pigment, cotton string; H 11 × W 2⅞ × D 2⅜ in.
National Cowboy Hall of Fame and Western Heritage Center,
Nicolai Fechin Collection

For the Hopi, the kachinas represent the sun, earth, wind, rain, and
other forces of nature. Depicted by ceremonial dancers, according to
tradition the kachinas live in the Hopi pueblos of northeast Arizona
half of the year before returning to their homes in the San Francisco
Mountains. The dancers give kachina dolls as gifts to children of the
pueblos, although during the twentieth century they also have been
made for sale.

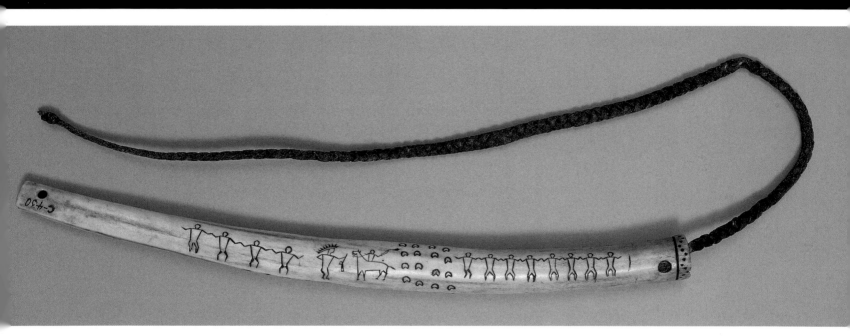

Blackfoot painting on canvas, Alberta

Canvas, pigments; 19½ × 18 in.; Glenbow Museum

In pre-reservation days, warriors depicted their war deeds on buffalo robes or tipi covers. Later, muslin and canvas obtained from traders or government issue were used to record important battles and individual valor.

Osage quirt, Southern Plains (ca. 1850)

Bone, braided leather; L 37⅜ × D 1 in.
Buffalo Bill Historical Center, Chandler-Pohrt Collection

Confrontation is seen in the carved figures of the standing and mounted warriors and their weapons.

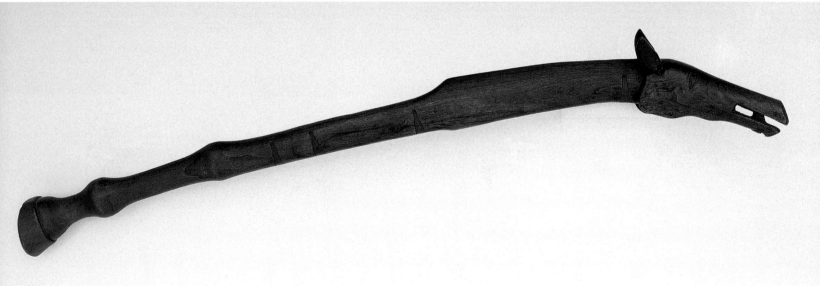

Annual Plains Indian Powwow, Buffalo Bill Historical Center
(June 1996)

Led by veterans carrying the eagle feathered staff and American and
Wyoming flags, dancers enter the arena during the Grand Entry.

Lakota horse dance stick, South Dakota (ca. 1890)
Wood, paint; L 35½ in.; Buffalo Bill Historical Center,
Adolf Spohr Collection, Gift of Larry Sheerin

CADZI CODY

Shoshone painted hide, Wyoming (ca. 1900)
Tanned cowhide, pigments; 60¾ × 55⅛ in.
Buffalo Bill Historical Center

During the early 1900s, Shoshone artist Cosiogo, working under the
name Cadzi Cody, produced nostalgic pre-reservation scenes of
buffalo hunting and other traditions. This painted hide has a central
Sun Dance scene surrounded by mounted warriors chasing buffalo.

Northern Plains warriors, to remind them of their abilities in capturing horses from enemy tribes or of other battle exploits.[17] Horse dance sticks also were made to honor favorite horses, which may have been killed or performed heroically in battle. The Lakota horse dance stick consists of a carved horse hoof for the handle and the horse head on the other end. In the middle of the stick are three triangular marks symbolizing the wounds suffered by the owner's horse in action.

Art as Cultural Identity and Survival

By the late 1870s, reservations had been established for the Plains tribes in Canada and the United States. The massacre of Lakota adherents to the Ghost Dance at Wounded Knee in December 1890 signaled the end of the old way of life. The people, however, made valiant efforts to preserve and protect their traditions, ceremonies and communities, despite the desperate conditions of the reservations. With the loss of the buffalo and the ability to freely hunt other game and to grow traditional foods, some ceremonies were altered. It is remarkable that so many communities and their traditions survived to the present.

During this period traditional materials, including decorated clothing, became increasingly important to people as a means of establishing their identities as Indians and as tribal members. Women also produced moccasins, clothing and other traditional objects as well as novelties for sale to individuals and through trading posts to augment family income during difficult times.

As tribes from the Eastern Woodlands came together with those from the Plains on reservations established in Indian Territory (present-day Oklahoma), styles were exchanged, and new trade materials led to creative innovations. The rise in popularity of the intertribal powwow after World War II provided the venue for the establishment of tribal clothing styles and northern and southern traditions. For some, powwow dancing is fundamental as a reflection of past traditions and a means of establishing contemporary identity as Indian people.

As native people seek to preserve, or, perhaps, regain their cultural heritages, they may seek out tribal objects in museum and personal collections as valuable links to the past. These objects provide continuity to the present, since they embody the philosophies, beliefs and changing lives of the people. In the words of Rick Hill:

Art is a way to express a people's struggle for cultural survival. Each generation's thinking about the world in which they find themselves is evidenced in the art of that culture. As new materials and new ideas came along, Indian artists reacted to the new stimuli. Ideas about art, culture, beauty and truth have always been evolving.[18]

The traditional art of Indian people may have many different meanings depending on one's point of view. For the museum curator or collector the object may be an example of fine craftsmanship, for the dealer a marketable product, or for the tourist a souvenir of a trip to the West. For native people today, the object speaks to the spirit and endurance of tribal cultures and provides a key to understanding the past, the present, the people who went before them, and their own generation.

Lakota storage bag, South Dakota (ca. 1890)
Buckskin, porcupine quills, tin cones, horse hair; 14³⁄₈ × 24¹⁄₄ in.
Buffalo Bill Historical Center, Chandler-Pohrt Collection

Ironically, during the late 1800s to early 1900s after the Plains tribes
had been confined to reservations, a flourishing of tribal arts
occurred. Porcupine quillwork, which preceded beadwork, continued
to be used, sometimes in combination with glass beads, fabric, tin
cones, or other trade materials.

Lakota pipe bag, South Dakota (ca. 1885)

Buckskin, glass beads, porcupine quills, canvas, rawhide; 39⅛ × 5⅞ in.
Buffalo Bill Historical Center, Chandler-Pohrt Collection,
Gift of Mr. and Mrs. Harold R. Tate

Lakota man's vest, South Dakota (ca. 1915)
Leather, beads; 20⅝ × 18½ in.
Buffalo Bill Historical Center, Gift of Mrs. Neill Phillips

For people on the reservations, traditional materials, including decorated clothing, became increasingly important as a means of establishing tribal identities. The Lakota excelled in producing distinctive fully beaded clothing, moccasins and other items, often with images of warriors and horses, cowboys, deer, elk, buffalo and other animals.

Lakota gauntlets, South Dakota (ca. 1925)

Buckskin, glass and brass beads; 16½ × 14½ in.; National Cowboy
Hall of Fame and Western Heritage Center, Joe Grandee Collection

As native economies suffered, traditional skills in hide work, quilling
and beading became sources of income for native women. Decorated
clothing was produced not only for personal use, but also for sale.

Salish handbag, Montana (ca. 1915)

Buckskin, glass beads, muslin, cotton cloth, metal; 10¼ × 7¾ in.

Buffalo Bill Historical Center, Gift of Mr. J.R. Simplot

Osage cradleboard, Oklahoma (ca. 1900)
Wood, brass tacks, beads, wool yarn, hawk bells, trade cloth;
42 × 11¼ in.
Buffalo Bill Historical Center, Chandler-Pohrt Collection

For native people, cradleboards provided safe places for babies
when families traveled or mothers worked. Distinctive designs were
adapted to tribal lifestyles and contain important cultural symbols.
For many tribes, the creation of cradleboards symbolized the joining
of two families, with members of each taking part.

Cheyenne cradleboard, Northern Plains (ca. 1890)
Buckskin, wood, beads, trade cloth, brass backs, cotton cloth; 47 × 13 in.
Buffalo Bill Historical Center, Adolf Spohr Collection,
Gift of Larry Sheerin

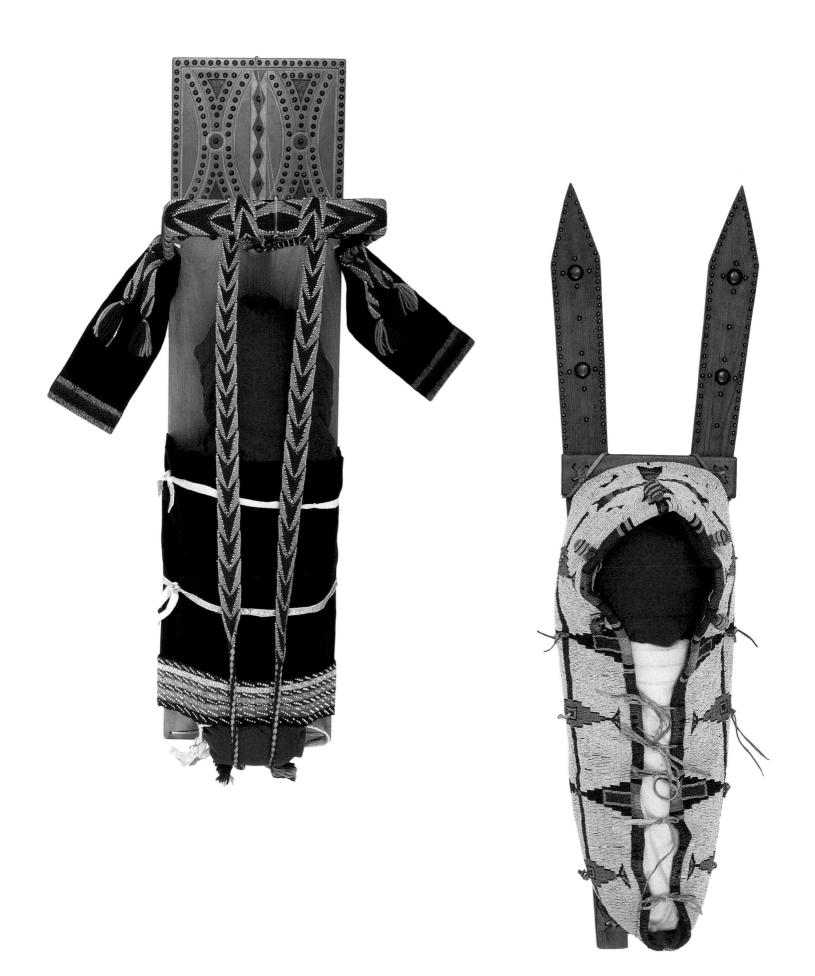

CECELIA YAZZIE

Navajo weaving (ca. 1980)

Wool, cotton; 37 × 34¾ in.; Autry Museum of Western Heritage

The artist depicts American astronauts on the moon with a spaceship
on a launch pad. According to Yazzie, her friends told her that this
was an inappropriate subject. She responded that she had visited
Kennedy Space Center and that the experience was part of her life,
that American Indians are a part of everyday events and activities in
the world around them.

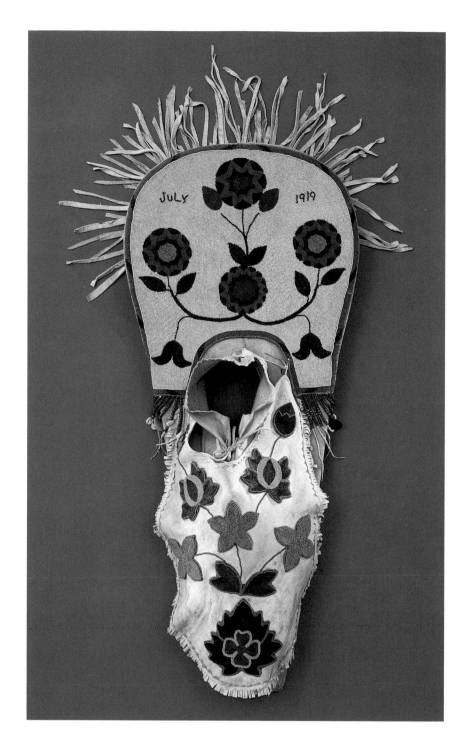

Salish cradleboard, Montana (ca. 1919)
Wood, buckskin, muslin, glass beads, cowrie shell, mother of pearl, abalone,
wool cloth, brass beads; 35 × 15 in.
Buffalo Bill Historical Center, Gift of J. R. Simplot

This cradleboard with its distinctive floral design and date of July 1919
was probably made for a special occasion such as a parade. During the
reservation period of the early 1900s, women enjoyed dressing themselves
and their horses in traditional attire for Fourth of July parades and tribal
celebrations. This practice continues today in such major events as the
Crow Fair held at Crow Agency, Montana every August.

1. For a demographic history of the populations of North American Indian Indians, see Russell Thornton, *American Indian Holocaust and Survival: A Population History Since 1492* (Norman: University of Oklahoma Press, 1987).

2. Bea Medicine, "The Anthropologist as the Indian's Image Maker," *Indian Historian*, 4, 1971.

3. See Richard West in *Creation's Journey: Native American Identity and Belief* (Washington, DC: Smithsonian Institution, 1984), p. 10. Also, Margaret Archuleta and Rennard Strickland, *Shared Visions: Native American Painters and Sculptors in the Twentieth Century* (Phoenix, AZ: The Heard Museum, 1991), and Bruce Bernstein and W. Jackson Rushing, *Modern by Tradition: American Indian Painting in the Studio Style* (Santa Fe: Museum of New Mexico Press, 1995), which describe the development of contemporary Indian art. The language used to describe American Indian art has been the subject of much debate among artists and art historians in recent years. In 1996, the Native Arts Network (ATLATL) titled its sixth biennial conference "We Have No Word for Art."

4. See Lloyd New in *Creativity Is Our Tradition: Three Decades of Contemporary Indian Art at the Institute of American Indian Arts* (Santa Fe, NM: Institute of American Indian Arts Press, 1992), p. 168.

5. Mary Jane Schneider, "Women's Work: An Examination of the Women's Roles in Plains Indian Arts and Crafts" in *The Hidden Half* (Washington, DC: University Press of America, Inc., 1983), pp. 101–122.

6. Interview with Birdie Burns, 1973.

7. Quoted in *Creativity Is Our Tradition*, p. 30.

8. N. Scott Momaday, *The Way to Rainy Mountain* (Albuquerque: University of New Mexico Press, 1969), p. 83.

9. Leslie Marmon Silko, "How to Write a Poem About the Sky," *Storyteller* (New York: Seaver Books, 1982), p. 177.

10. For more detailed descriptions and analysis of rock art, see James D. Keyser, "A Lexicon for Historic Plains Indian Rock Art: Increasing Interpretive Potential," *Plains Anthropologist*, 1987, Vol.32, No. 115, pp. 43–72; and Lawrence L. Loendorf and Stuart W. Conner, "The Pectol Shields and the Shield-Bearing Warrior Rock Art Motif," *Journal of California and Great Basin Anthropology*, 1993, Vol. 15, No. 2, pp. 216–224.

11. George Bird Grinnell, *The Cheyenne Indians: Their History and Ways of Life*, Vol. 2 (New Haven: Yale University Press, 1923), pp. 96, 148.

12. See George Catlin, *O-KEE-PA: A Religious Ceremony and Other Customs of the Mandans* (New Haven: Yale University Press, 1967), and Roy W. Meyer, *The Village Indians of the Upper Missouri: The Mandans, Hidatsas, and Arikaras* (Lincoln: University of Nebraska Press, 1977).

13. Interview with Ben Calf Rope, Siksika, Glenbow Museum Archives, Glenbow Museum, Calgary, Alberta, Canada.

14. Quoted in James Mooney, *The Ghost-Dance Religion and the Sioux Outbreak of 1890* (Chicago: University of Chicago Press, 1965), p. 245.

15. Mooney, *The Ghost-Dance Religion and the Sioux Outbreak of 1890*, p. 222.

16. See Lois Essary Jacka, *Beyond Tradition: Contemporary Indian Art and Its Evolution* (Flagstaff, AZ: Northland Publishing Company,1988), p. 12.

17. John C. Ewers, *Plains Indian Sculpture* (Washington, DC: Smithsonian Institution Press, 1986), pp. 139–152.

18. Rick Hill, *Creativity Is Our Tradition*, pp. 46–47.

Frozen in Time

Euro-American Portrayals of Indians

SARAH E. BOEHME

W HEN EUROPEANS FIRST BEGAN DEVELOPING THEIR CONCEPTS OF North America, visual representations of the native inhabitants became an important part of portraying the continent.[1] Pictures of the people whose appearances, customs and clothing were unfamiliar and exotic served as symbols of the mysterious land.[2]

A geographical error caused Europeans to apply the name "Indian" to the diverse peoples who lived on the North American continent. This misnomenclature reminds us that the identification was imposed by people outside the native cultures. Similarly, the numerous paintings and sculptures of native peoples produced by Euro-American artists are constructed from a vantage point outside the culture being depicted. The way that native peoples are portrayed often reveals more about the portrayer than the subject. In discussing the Euro-American imagery, the use of the term "Indian" to refer to the native peoples is evocative of this constructed identity.[3]

Today, most works of art with American Indian subjects are associated with the regional subset of Western American art.[4] In art of this continent's Western regions, the images of American Indians are important in the artistic iconography. Portraits, scenes of American Indian life, historical narratives including Indians—all feature prominently in the art held by collectors and museums of the West.[5]

Juxtaposing art about American Indians with art by American Indians provides new insights. As Emma Hansen has pointed out, "North American Indian languages have no equivalent word for 'art.'"[6] In American Indian cultures, the result of object-making is an item that functions in either in a very practical or a cultural sense. The counterpoint to that approach of object-making is exemplified in the twentieth-century American concept of art, which is rooted in late nineteenth-century Euro-American culture. In that context, the arts generate objects honored for decorative and aesthetic qualities. The catch phrase "art for art's sake" summarizes the belief that art is at its highest point when it is valued for itself, not for functional purposes. This aesthetic stance, stressing the essential visual elements, is related to the high value placed on progress in the Euro-American culture. The arts progress by becoming more purely artistic.

GEORGE CATLIN (1796–1872)

Eh-toh'k-pah-she-pée-shah, The Black Moccasin, Hidatsa

Oil on canvas; 28¼ × 22¾ in.; Gilcrease Museum (0126.2179)

Although Catlin sought to keep the paintings in his Indian Gallery
together, he also painted additional versions of his original subjects
resulting in works such as this portrait of an aged Hidatsa leader.
Although his gallery of images included many portraits of young,
vibrant Indian subjects, Catlin made certain to include portrayals
of wise, venerable patriarchs.

The Euro-American cultural emphasis on "art for art's sake" values creativity, individuality and aesthetics. One intellectual danger in the theory of "art for art's sake" is that the concept obscures the roles that art plays in culture. No matter what the emphasis on aesthetics, art performs other functions. By emphasizing only aesthetic qualities, subject matter is not evaluated for the content it carries. This essay will look at the representations of American Indian subjects in Euro-American art and consider the larger function these images played.

Place in the Universe: Contributions to Science

In the early nineteenth century, artists who recorded images of American Indians were motivated by an impulse to understand the world by describing and categorizing it. Europeans' views of the world were changed with the encounter with the North American continent, which was a discovery for that culture. A belief in the rational ordering of the universe and the growth of the discipline of science required the gathering and dissemination of information and knowledge. The function of describing is especially important when the viewer has little knowledge of the subject, as is the case with American Indians depicted by non-Indian artists. Working in an American society which was only beginning to develop a national art, Euro-American artists cited the primary value of their Indian paintings as documentary. Artist George Catlin, who traveled the West in the 1830s, explained that he had devoted himself to the "production of a literal and graphic delineation of the living manners, customs, and character of an interesting race of people . . . who have no historians or biographers of their own to pourtray with fidelity their native looks and history."[7] Discounting native forms of oral history and biography, Catlin saw his mission as gathering information in both visual and written forms that would be accessible and valued by his own culture. The artist first went through the process of learning for himself by creating images. Catlin reported that painting Indian subjects was a way of knowing more about these people.[8]

The knowledge gathered by the individual artist through the artistic process then became information that could be communicated to an audience through exhibitions and publications. Although artists often reported on the responses of American Indians to their portraits, it must be remembered that almost all depictions of Native American peoples were intended to be viewed by non–Native American audiences. The information conveyed gave the viewer knowledge of a culture outside his/her own. The paintings and sculpture of American artists usually required a textual accompaniment. Verbal descriptions of unfamiliar material are abstract. Visual descriptions offer a replication of the process of seeing and give the viewer access only to information about appearances. Both text and image were needed to convey information about the unfamiliar. Thus artists often accompanied their visual documentation with written documentation. George Catlin's publication *Letters and Notes on the Manners, Customs and Conditions of the North American Indians* provided written explanations of the scenes he portrayed and biographical details related to his portraits. These two forms of communication, written and visual, reinforced each other.

Individual works of art were also reinforced by other works of art. To describe Indians fully it was necessary to have an accumulation of information. Images of native peoples often appeared as parts of series or collections. Catlin compiled his images of Indians in an Indian Gallery, which he struggled to keep together against all odds.[9] The burgeoning scientific disciplines provided a model for looking at information which was classified and ordered.

The linking of American Indian images to science appears even more explicit in the work of Swiss artist Karl Bodmer, who was brought to the American continent by Prince Maximilian of Wied, a natural historian by avocation.[10] Maximilian's concern for documenting demanded detailed accuracy.

In conjunction with gathering information on Indian tribes, artists asserted that this information was especially valuable because it preserved a vanishing race. John Mix Stanley followed Catlin's lead and created an Indian Gallery filled with portraits and genre scenes. In the preface to the catalogue for his Gallery, Stanley concluded that he hoped that his paintings would interest the visitors and "excite some desire that the memory, at least, of these tribes may not become extinct."[11] Stanley's allegorical painting *Last of Their Race* portrays this belief that the tribes faced extinction. The painting depicts remnants of different tribes pushed to the edge of the Pacific Ocean with the sun setting in the distance and a buffalo skull as an emblem of death in the foreground. Stanley painted this work after serving as artist with an expedition mapping a possible route for a transcontinental railroad and it was owned by the leader of that expedition, Isaac I. Stevens.[12] The artist's experiences must have made him aware of effects that the expanding United States would have on the native peoples. The melancholy tone of the painting suggests regret and sympathy for the Indians, but the work is, nevertheless, an acceptance of the inevitability of the demise.

The Indian Gallery is usually considered an early nineteenth-century phenomenon, exemplified by Catlin's traveling galleries. The approach, however, was echoed in the latter part of the nineteenth century as artists such as Joseph Henry Sharp and E. A. Burbank developed massive collections of American Indian portraiture, which had links to ethnographic study. Their forays into Indian portraiture began in the late nineteenth century, after the conclusion of the United States military encounters with tribes in the West (often called the Indian wars). The artists sought out the old warriors, the Indian leaders of the past. The late nineteenth-century artists often had private patrons who commissioned works, so the artists were not as personally motivated to keep and exhibit their own Indian galleries. Sharp followed the model of anthropologists by moving from his home base of Cincinnati to the West to live among the American Indian people he wanted to portray. He settled on the Crow Indian reservation in Montana, where he sought to portray Indian customs at the same time that the United States government was suppressing traditional customs to encourage Indians to assimilate. His patrons included Phoebe Hearst, who bought portraits for an anthropological museum, and the United States government, which acquired eleven portraits for the Smithsonian.[13]

Artist Elbridge A. Burbank (1858–1949) also had private patronage that was amassing work for what would become a museum collection.[14] He was commissioned to paint Indian portraits by his uncle Edward E. Ayer, president of the Field Museum and a founder of the Newbery Library. His portraits, often quite detailed in representing costumes and facial features, have an inanimate character, as if they were specimens.

Despite the many portraits created in Indian galleries and in other series done for anthropological reasons, only a few American Indians are easily identifiable by non-Indians. The names often cited are associated with the Indian wars—Sitting Bull and Geronimo.[15] Spurred by newspaper accounts of the Apache Geronimo's conflicts with the United States military in the Southwest, Burbank traveled to Fort Sill, where Geronimo was imprisoned, to paint a portrait which the artist then copied numerous times. The replication that Burbank

Karl Bodmer (1809–1893), artist
Louis René Lucien Rollet (1809–1862), engraver
**Pehriska-Ruhpa, Moennitari Warrior in the Costume of the Dog
Danse, drawn ca. 1834, engraved 1840–43**
Engraving and aquatint (hand colored); 24⁷⁄₈ × 18⅛ in.
Buffalo Bill Historical Center, Gift of Clara S. Peck (21.69.23)

Pehriska-Puhpa was a Minnatarre, or Hidatsa, leader whom Bodmer
and Maximilian met when they stayed at Fort Clark in the winter of
1834. Bodmer painted a watercolor sketch of Pehriska-Ruhpa in his
Dog Dance clothing, and later prepared the image for engraving
and set the pose to show a dance posture. Because Bodmer was an
eyewitness, his works are often cited for their authentic portrayals.
Ethnologists today continue to value this image, for the sharp focus
realism and striking example of Indian portraiture.

JOHN MIX STANLEY (1814–1872)

Last of Their Race (1857)

Oil on canvas; 43 × 60 in.; Buffalo Bill Historical Center (5.75)

Stanley, following in the footsteps of Catlin, created an Indian Gallery comprised of portraits from his extensive travels in the West. Created apart from his Gallery, this allegorical painting of the demise of the Indian race drew upon the artist's knowledge of different Indian peoples. Stanley portrayed the remnants of diverse tribes pushed to the edge of the Pacific Ocean.

D. B. ROBINSON (active 1875–1876)

Sapo-Omock-Sokah (ca. 1875–76)

Watercolor; 15¼ × 11⅝ in.

Glenbow Museum (991.20.1). Purchased with funds from the Glenbow Museum Acquisitions Society and with a repatriation grant from the Canadian Cultural Property Export Review Board, Department of Communications, Government of Canada, 1991

Canada also witnessed an artistic interest in the compiling of Indian portraiture. A young English amateur artist about whom little is known, Robinson traveled to Toronto where he became friends with Col. James Macleod, who was in charge of the North-West Mounted Police. Robinson then journeyed to the Far West to visit Macleod, hunt and paint Indian portraits, such as this sensitive portrayal of Chief Crowfoot, a Blackfeet.

JOSEPH HENRY SHARP (1859–1953)

White Swan (ca. 1904)

Oil on canvas; 17⅝ × 11¾ in.

Buffalo Bill Historical Center, Whitney Purchase Fund (18.61)

Sharp moved to the West, establishing homes in Montana and New Mexico, in order to live among the subjects he wanted to portray. His approach paralleled that of anthropologists who sought to immerse themselves in Indian cultures. Sharp wanted to portray what he believed was the authentic Indian, personified by the warriors of the Indian wars, such as White Swan. A Crow, White Swan was best known among the American audience as a scout for Lt. Col. George Custer, although among his own people he was noted for accomplishments in other intertribal conflicts.

ELBRIDGE AYER BURBANK (1858–1949)

Chief Geronimo, Apache

Oil on canvas; 12¼ × 10⅛ in.; Eiteljorg Museum of American Indians and Western Art, Gift of Harrison Eiteljorg

Burbank's Indian portraits were commissioned by the artist's uncle, Edward Ayer, president of the Field Museum in Chicago. The compiling of Indian likenesses was again seen as part of a scientific investigation. Geronimo's fame seemed to derive from the popular press, which avidly promoted stories of his resistance to capture. Geronimo continues to be one of the few Indian persons identifiable by white audiences.

EDWARD S. CURTIS (1868–1952), photographer
JOHN ANDREW & SON, printer
Cheyenne Warriors (from 1905 copyright photograph)
Photogravure; 22 × 18 in.
Buffalo Bill Historical Center, Gift of Douglas L. Manship

Curtis produced the equivalent of an Indian gallery in the
photographic medium with his massive publication of Indian
photographs, the twenty-four-volume *The North American Indian:
Being a Series of Volumes Picturing and Describing the Indians of
the United States and Alaska.* The photograph, with its convincing
replication of reality, made Curtis' work seem more truthful than
painted representations. Recent research has demonstrated, however,
that Curtis invented many of his images by selecting clothing and
setting poses of his subjects.

NICHOLAS DE GRANDMAISON (1892–1978)
Indian Chief
Pastel on paper; 18 7/16 × 14 in.; Glenbow Museum,
from the Collection of James and Eva Mahaffey,
a bequest of Eva Mildred Mahaffey, 1990 (990.66.2)

De Grandmaison's pastel portraits brought the concept of the Indian
gallery into the early twentieth century. The "chief" with an
impressive feathered war bonnet remains a staple image.

CHARLES BIRD KING (1785–1862)
Peahmuska, A Fox Chief (1824)
*Oil on wood panel; 17 3/8 × 13 7/8 in.; Eiteljorg Museum of American
Indians and Western Art, Gift of Harrison Eiteljorg*

This portrait is one of several of Peahmuska that King painted. The
first version was painted for the Indian Gallery being compiled by
Thomas L. McKenney, the first head of the governmental department
which became the Bureau of Indian Affairs. McKenney originally
commissioned the portrait when Peahmuska came to Washington,
D.C., with a delegation of Fox in the summer of 1824. McKenney's
Gallery was on exhibit in the Smithsonian in 1865, when a fire
destroyed the collection. King's copies of his own paintings, such
as this one, preserved some of the images.

produced, however, still reached only limited audiences. Geronimo's fame or notoriety did not became widespread until he became the subject of popular media such as film.

The Indian Gallery concept found a new medium at the end of the century with the development of photography. Edward S. Curtis took his camera where formerly artists had carried brushes and paint. He compiled his portraits in a massive publication, grouped by tribes, but tellingly introduced by an image entitled *The Vanishing Race*. Curtis's evocative, elegant portraits have become some of the most widely known visual images. The verisimilitude of the photographic image has made them seem hallmarks of authenticity. Curtis, however, posed many of his figures and erased evidence of modern life.

In the twentieth century the tradition of developing large-scale collections of American Indian portraits has continued. The vanishing race concept has a new element. The race was seen as threatened not only with extinction but also with dilution. Artist Nicholas de Grandmaison exemplifies the concern for finding the authentic Indian. As stated by de Grandmaison's biographer, "What he sought were 'pure' Indians whose faces showed no strain of Scottish, French or other European heritage." [16] His concept of what an Indian was, was inspired by a romantic ideal, which he believed was reflected in the faces of the authentic Indian. He posed his subjects in traditional clothing, omitting references to contemporary life. Although artists like de Grandmaison painted portraits, the individual identities of the subjects were not paramount. The seeking of knowledge through the recording of images satisfies a psychological motivation of curiosity. Knowledge, however, has often meant power.

Recording History

The recording of historical moments has been another important motivation in the creation of Indian images. The history of the United States has closely been tied to the history of expansion of the nation across the continent. Canadian history has offered an interesting parallel. Portraits painted in the early nineteenth century of Indians who made state visits to Washington, D.C., served as commemorations of important events. In these instances, the works were not created for the Indians who posed for them. The paintings were intended to reside in the government's care, as part of an archive which would be maintained by the department of Indian Affairs. The portraits often included images of assimilated Indians, such as Charles Bird King's portrait of David Vann, but these have not been valued as highly as those of the exotic Indians. Their lack of distinguishing Indianness makes them appear inauthentic.

Since the European Renaissance, history painting, which portrays human activity, was considered the most noble form of art making. Although American artists appear to eschew the theoretical preoccupation with hierarchies of types of depictions, they nevertheless have inherited the tradition which places their narratives in a context of human accomplishment. Those accomplishments have traditionally included a vanquishing of enemies. Thus Indians became the foil, the enemy worthy of conquest. Carl Wimar, a German immigrant painter, depicted *The Abduction of Boone's Daughters*, a painting whose subject of treachery parallels the literary genre of captivity story.

Custer's Last Stand became one of the most widely portrayed scenes in American history. Custer served as an heroic figure who stood for bravery and, most importantly, sacrifice. His projected nobility required an antithesis, and the Sioux and Cheyenne warriors who battled successfully against the Seventh Cavalry provided material for the artistic contrast. Crude drawings for newspapers became fine arts paintings, which were then reproduced in prints and posters which were widely distributed.

Although Custer's Last Stand was the most popular single subject, the image of the wild Indian at battle has reappeared in many guises. In contemporary Western art the savage Indian continues to hold a prominent place. The recording of battles also points to the importance of conflict and resolution. Dramatic confrontations of culture against culture and the catharsis of resolution appear frozen in narrative paintings, but take their most powerful form in the filmed images of the twentieth century.

The foe in representations of battles reinforced the prominence of the Indian warrior. Early nineteenth-century artists such as Catlin and Bodmer had usually sought to represent in their portraits the most important members within a tribe, searching out "chiefs" and those who had status. Depicting many tribes, these artists sought to portray the clothing and personal adornment of individuals and thus their paintings did include distinctions between the tribes. With the emphasis on the Indian as the enemy, the warrior nature was symbolized by the readily identifiable feathered headgear. As shorthand, this one item of apparel, which combines beauty with meaning, became the ultimate symbol of all Indians, even though it has no relevance to many American Indian tribes. The different cultures of the Southwest and the Northwest are ignored in a concentration on the Plains Indians.[17] The portrayal of buffalo hunting as practiced by Plains Indians also takes a moment in history and makes it stand for all Indian cultures. This theme in painting and sculpture also often signals the vanishing race theme because the human Indian is linked with the bison, which was also nearly exterminated.

While paintings often present narratives such as battle or hunting scenes, sculpture often represents an iconic image. The Indian on horseback has been interpreted and reinterpreted. In Western art, the cowboy is often depicted struggling against the wild nature of the horse in representations of the bucking bronco. Indian subjects often appear unified with their horses, as in Frederic Remington's *The Cheyenne*, which signifies the concept of the Indian as a savage who races across the plains.

The best-known Indian equestrian representation, James Earle Fraser's *End of the Trail* (frontispiece), encapsulates the concept of the Indian as vanishing race. Fraser modeled the monumental version of this sculpture for the Pan-Pacific Exposition in 1915, then produced smaller editions in bronze, which brought the image to additional audiences.[18] Fraser created an icon for the vanishing race concept that is masterful in its simplicity. The dejected Indian, seated on a horse whose posture echoes the melancholy theme, inverts the usually heroic formula of the equestrian sculpture. The sculptural medium, which is three-dimensional, focuses on the figure in isolation. The content, carried in the silhouette's simplicity, has engendered many replications in different materials from prints to beadwork.

Historical moments when cultures came together peacefully often depict the progress of the white culture, as in Sacagawea's aiding the exploring party led by Lewis and Clark. Sacagawea, the most frequently portrayed Indian woman in Western art, guides the exploring party as they survey the Western territories. She adds an exotic touch, and a maternal one, as she is often portrayed in her role as mother to her child born on the journey.

TOMPKINS MATTESON (1813–1884)

Battle of the Little Big Horn (1878)

Oil on canvas; 27⅞ × 37 1/16 in.; Autry Museum of Western Heritage

Matteson's painting is one of thousands produced on the subject
of the Battle of the Little Bighorn. The most common form of the
iconography presents Custer taking a "last stand." Custer and his
soldiers are portrayed in a defensive stance, making a final doomed
stand and bravely facing attacking Indians. This iconography
creates an heroic Custer, who serves as an emblem of the soldier
who offers himself in sacrifice. Thus the paintings of Custer's Last
Stand become part of the contested terrain of what really happened
at the Little Bighorn.

49

Otto Becker (1854–1945), lithographer

Cassily Adams (1843–1921), artist

Custer's Last Fight (1896)

Colored lithograph; 30½ × 42½ in.

Buffalo Bill Historical Center, Gift of The Coe Foundation (1.69.420A)

This print is probably the best known visual interpretation of the
battle of the Little Bighorn, and, in fact, might be one of the best
known images in American art due to the wide distribution of
this print. Adams painted his version of Custer's Last Stand in the
1880s and it hung in a St. Louis saloon, which was acquired by the
Anheuser-Busch brewing company. Anheuser-Busch then produced
a lithographic print of the painting and gave prints to their
distributors, bars and other outlets. Through its display in bars,
it became widely known by diverse audiences.

50

FREDERIC REMINGTON (1861–1909)
The Cheyenne (1902)
Bronze, cast number 9; height 21⅛ × base length 14½ × base width
7¼ in.; Buffalo Bill Historical Center,
Gift of Mrs. Henry H. R. Coe, (17.71)

Seeking images for his paintings and sculpture, Remington traveled
in the West, often in the company of military troops who were
engaged in conflicts with Indian tribes. The artist greatly admired
military life and the role of battles in testing and proving an
individual's worth. Because of this vantage point, Remington saw,
and portrayed, Indian subjects as wild savages, the enemy. Yet he
also admired Indian fortitude and warrior skills.

HENRY LION (1900–1966)

Lewis and Clark and Sacagawea (ca. 1963)

Bronze; height 35¼ × base width 28¼ × base length 25¼ in.

Buffalo Bill Historical Center, Gift of Charles S. Jones (27.64)

This sculpture commemorates the exploration of the territory
acquired by the United States government through the Louisiana
Purchase. The leaders of the exploring party, Meriwether Lewis and
William Clark, are aided by the Shoshone woman Sacagawea, whose
presence confers an acceptance of the goals of the exploring party.

Cultural Identity

In Euro-American culture, the concept of fine arts is a mark of cultural identity. Contrast between cultures is implicit in many Euro-American representations of American Indian subject matter. In a painting such as Seth Eastman's *The Tanner*, an Indian woman is tanning a skin, seemingly a straightforward representation of everyday life. Texts by Mary Eastman, the artist's wife, however, interpret this scene as a representation of the hard life of Indian women, of a never-ceasing labor which signifies the condition of women in Indian tribes. According to Mary Eastman, "A degraded state of woman is universally characteristic of savage life." [19]

In contrast to Eastman's painting, American Indian women have sometimes been represented as objects of desire. Such interpretations serve to reinforce ideas of cultural superiority. Negative stereotypes in popular culture, such as the drunken Indian, appear far less commonly in the fine arts of painting and sculpture, which tend to portray ideals rather than imperfections.

This emphasis on comparisons between cultures can also point to desirable qualities. American Indians have come to symbolize communion with nature, in an evocation of a simpler world. Early nineteenth-century written accounts, such as those by George Catlin, identified the Indian as a primitive man, whose life was in harmony with the natural world. This concept of the Noble Savage undergirded many representations, such Joseph Henry Sharp's painting *Great Mystery—Moonlight*. This notion of the Indian as the primitive man echoes the formulation of the eighteenth-century philosopher Jean Jacques Rousseau. The Noble Savage, the man who is elemental, free and natural, contrasts sharply with modern man, who is seen as burdened and disengaged from nature. Works of art are often created to provide ideals for the viewer. As aesthetic objects, paintings and sculpture have often been created to provide beauty and visual enhancement. The figure in *Great Mystery—Moonlight* portrays ideals of the perfectly formed human body, which echoes representations from Greek and Roman art.

Economic Motivations

An obvious motivation underlies the creation of most works of art, the creation of objects of economic value, which can be traded or sold for necessities or enhanced status. In nineteenth and early twentieth century society of the United States and Canada, the growing leisure classes with accumulated wealth provided a market for works of art. Euro-American artists found that Indian subjects sell. Joseph Henry Sharp noted that his painting of landscapes sold better if he included a tepee in them. E. I. Couse, his contemporary in the artist colony in Taos, New Mexico, found a formula that proved popular. He depicted a single Indian contemplating a cultural object, such as a basket or a pot. His paintings interpreted American Indians as creators of works of art themselves. The paintings also often highlighted the types of American Indian art—basketry, pottery, weavings—which were beginning to be collected. Yet the subjects of the paintings did not necessarily share in the economic benefits, often posing for nominal sums of money. One contemporary artist commented that he was told by an art dealer that a portrait of a chief in a headdress would fetch more money than portraits of other types of Westerners. [20]

S ETH E ASTMAN (1808–1875)
The Tanner (1848)
Oil on canvas; 30³/₁₆ × 25¹/₄ in.
Rockwell Museum, Gift of Robert F. Rockwell, Jr. (78.29 F)

Eastman, an officer in the United States Army, painted scenes of the
Indian life near Fort Snelling in Minnesota territory, where he was
stationed. Because he lived near the Dakota and Chippewa people,
Eastman was able to observe and then depict many aspects of
everyday life, instead of only visiting Indian tribes for brief periods
as many of his contemporaries commonly did. His plain style and
seemingly unstudied compositions make his paintings seem to be
factual and realistic, but the texts that accompanied illustrations of
his work added interpretations which included moral judgements
of Indian cultures.

JOHN CLYMER (1907–1989)

Tribal Hunt (1972)

Oil on canvas; 30 × 40 in.; National Museum of Wildlife Art

Twentieth-century Western American art continues to depict Indians
as they lived in the past. The popular subject of the buffalo hunt
links Indian people with the bison, an animal which was almost
exterminated and thus connects the Indian with the idea of doomed
fate.

Joseph Henry Sharp (1859–1953)
The Great Mystery—Moonlight
Oil on canvas; 30 × 40 in.; Gilcrease Museum

Sharp wrote, "The Indian reverence for the Great Spirit is universal.
They go to the mountains to fast and pray for their 'medicine' and
guidance." While he recognized the importance of spiritual concerns
in Indian cultures, Sharp's designation of a "universal" spirituality,
coupled with his romantic representation of an Indian mediating on
mystery, presents a positive stereotype.

DAVE McGARY (b. 1958)

American Horse (1992)

Painted bronze, cast number 28 of 30; height 40 × width 19¼ × 20 in.

Buffalo Bill Historical Center, Gift of Paul and Joan Gelhausen and Family:

Dana, Chandler and Alicia (8.94)

Contemporary Western art also includes representations by Euro-American artists which venerate specific Indian persons, as in this portrait of American Horse (1840–1908), an Oglala Sioux. The artist researched the biography of his subject and portrayed American Horse in clothing that identified him as Indian (war bonnet), but also included evidence of contact with the Euro-American culture (the blue cloth shirt). Yet Indian history has so often been constructed by external cultures that questions will be asked about who should now be presenting the history of Indian peoples.

The fascination with American Indian subject matter in American art, and particularly in the region of the American West, has kept the subject prominent, yet has tended to present the American Indian as a figure frozen in time. Henry Farny's *Days of Long Ago* serves as an example. The title places the subject in non-specific time, yet these Indians who live peacefully with their tepees blending into the natural setting serve as the model for who and what Indians are. Works of art are powerful because the images are beautiful or visually engaging. They create ideals which can ossify into positive stereotypes, which can be as limiting as negative stereotypes. Although the representation of American Indians has varied throughout the last two centuries, the similarities are often more important than the differences. The same ways of representing American Indian subjects appear again and again. The persistence of these images indicates the powerful hold they have. The examination of those images and their cultural meanings can, however, lead to new understandings.

1. As curator of the painting and sculpture collections at the Buffalo Bill Historical Center, I will follow the recommendation of this museum's Plains Indian Advisory Board, which has recorded a preference for the term "American Indian" over "Native American." Consequently, I will use the word "Indian" to refer to the peoples who were the first inhabitants of the continent and their descendants. Minutes of the Plains Indian Advisory Board Held June 23, 1994. The terminology also serves a purpose in this essay.

2. Hugh Honour, *The New Golden Land: European Images of America from the Discoveries to the Present Time* (New York: Pantheon Books, 1976).

3. Julie Schimmel, "Inventing the Indian," in William H. Truettner, ed., *The West as America: Reinterpreting Images of the Frontier, 1820–1920* (Washington, D.C., and London: Smithsonian Institution Press, for the National Museum of American Art, 1991).

4. The Indian has been seen as an appropriate subject for American artists at different points in the nation's art history. See Elwood Parry, *The Image of the Indian and the Black in American Art* (New York: G. Braziller, 1974).

5. The subject of this exhibition, for example, grew from discussions among directors, curators and educators from the staffs of the Museums West organization about commonality in their collections.

6. Emma I. Hansen, "Persistent Voices: Art of the Plains and Southwest," page 5 of this publication.

7. George Catlin, *Letters and Notes of the Manners, Customs and Conditions of the North American Indians . . . Written during Eight Years' Travel amongst the Wildest Tribes of Indians in North America* (London: Published by the author at Egyptian Hall, 1841), I, 3.

8. Catlin, *Letters and Notes Indians*, I, 2.

9. On Catlin's gallery and the relationship of his work to the American scientific community, see William H. Truettner, *The Natural Man Observed: A Study of Catlin's Indian Gallery* (Washington, D.C.: Smithsonian Institution Press, 1979). Also, Brian W. Dippie, *Catlin and His Contemporaries: The Politics of Patronage* (Lincoln and London: The University of Nebraska Press, 1990), and Joan Carpenter Troccoli, *First Artist of the West: George Catlin Paintings and Watercolors from the Collection of Gilcrease Museum* (Tulsa: Gilcrease Museum, 1993).

10. Maximilian published his written account of the journey accompanied with prints made from Bodmer's watercolors. For an accessible English edition, see Maximilian, Prince of Wied, *Travels in the Interior of North America, 1832–1834*, vols. 24–24 of *Early Western Travels, 1748–1846*, ed. Reuben Gold Thwaites (Cleveland: Arthur H. Clark Co., 1906). On Bodmer, see William H. Goetzmann, David C. Hunt, Marsha Gallagher and William J. Orr, *Karl Bodmer's America* (Omaha: Joslyn Art Museum, 1984).

11. John Mix Stanley, *Portraits of North American Indians, with Sketches of Scenery, etc. Painted by J. M. Stanley, Deposited with The Smithsonian Institution* (Washington: Smithsonian Institution, 1852), n.p.

12. *Reports of Explorations and Surveys to Ascertain the Most Practicable and Economic Route for a Railroad from the Mississippi River to the Pacific Ocean*, Isaac I. Stevens, Northern Route, vol. 12, 1960.

E. I. COUSE (1866–1936)

The Sand Painter (1927)

*Oil on canvas; 27 ½ × 35 ½ in.; National Cowboy Hall of Fame and
Western Heritage Center, Gift of Jasper D. Ackerman (A.029.2)*

Couse's paintings celebrate Indian creativity through the
representation of the artistic productions. The artist settled in Taos,
New Mexico, which in the early twentieth century became a colony
for artists interested in depicting Indian life. The Taos artists were
often cited by art critics who reviewed their exhibitions as producers
of truly American art because their subject matter represented
uniquely American subjects, the Native Americans.

59

HENRY FARNY (1847–1916)

Days of Long Ago (1903)

Oil on board; 37½ × 23¾ in.; Buffalo Bill Historical Center (6.75)

The high horizon and shadowy, sheltering trees form an intimate
setting for Farny's family group. With the title *Days of Long Ago*,
Farny wistfully places the scene in some distant, but not specific time.
His painting reinforces the idea of Indians living in harmony with
nature.

JAMES BAMA (b. 1926)
A Contemporary Sioux (1978)
Oil on panel; 23 ⅜ × 35 ⅜ in.; Buffalo Bill Historical Center,
William E. Weiss Contemporary Fund Purchase (19.78)

In contemporary Western art, Indian people are often portrayed
as living in the past. Using a realistic style, Bama portrayed a
contemporary Indian who maintains a relationship with the past,
but also needs to find his place in contemporary society, which is
dominated by the culture of white persons. The message on the wall
behind the young Sioux man echoes the theme of the lack of place
for Indians in mainstream American society.

61

13. For Sharp, see Forrest Fenn, *The Beat of the Drum and the Whoop of the Dance: A Study of the Life and Work of Joseph Henry Sharp* (Santa Fe, New Mexico: Fenn Publishing Company, 1983). For his life in Montana, see Sarah E. Boehme, *Absarokee Hut: The Joseph Henry Sharp Cabin* (Cody, WY: Buffalo Bill Historical Center, 1992).

14. E. A. Burbank as told to Ernest Royce, ed. by Frank J. Taylor, *Burbank Among the Indians* (Caldwell, ID: The Caxton Printers, Ltd., 1946).

15. Formative evaluation surveys conducted by the Education Department, Autry Museum of Western Heritage.

16. Hugh A. Dempsey, *History in Their Blood: The Indian Portraits of Nicholas de Grandmaison* (New York: Hudson Hills Press, 1982), p. 19.

17. John C. Ewers, "The Emergence of the Plains Indian as the Symbol of the North American Indian," *Annual Report of the Smithsonian Institution*, 1964, pp. 531–544.

18. The plaster made for the Exposition is now in the collection of the National Cowboy Hall of Fame, Oklahoma City, Oklahoma. For the story of Fraser's sculpture, see Dean Krakel, *End of the Trail: The Odyssey of a Statue* (Norman: University of Oklahoma Press, 1973).

19. Mary Eastman, *Dahcotah; or Life and Legends of the Sioux around Fort Snelling*, preface by Mrs. C. M. Kirkland, illustrated by drawings by Captain Eastman (New York: John Wiley, 1849), 11. For Eastman, see also Sarah E. Boehme, Christian F. Feest and Patricia Condon Johnson, *Seth Eastman: A Portfolio of North American Indians* (Afton, MN: Afton Historical Press, 1995).

20. *The Art of James Bama*, text by Elmer Kelton (New York: Bantam Books, 1993), p. 133.

History, Connections and Cultural Renewal

GERALD T. CONATY

CLIFFORD CRANE BEAR

*T*he history of western North America has provided both Canada and the United States with some of their most powerful national images. In the United States, portrayals of pitched battles between the First Peoples and the newcomers—along with the icon of the lone, independent, idiosyncratic mountain man—have, in many ways, defined the national persona and the struggle to overcome the wilderness.[1] Alternatively, the Canadian identity as reasonable and compromising arises from the dominance of disciplined, corporate adventurers employed by the Hudson's Bay Company and from the peaceable negotiations of the North-West Mounted Police (now known as the Royal Canadian Mounted Police). And, of course, the image of the skilled Plains warrior destined for extinction as progress overcomes his unfettered life provides justification and a sense of the inevitable to the events of the late nineteenth century.

But the images of the West which most of us have received are only one side of a multi-faceted history. When we look more closely at historical events, it becomes clear that Natives and newcomers have had very different understandings of them. In many cases, these episodes have been key in shaping how the West was developed, and the differing perspectives of them have formed the foundations of the relationships between Natives and non-Natives. This is especially true when issues of land and land ownership are concerned.

The treaties signed between the First Peoples and the Euro-American and Euro-Canadian newcomers comprise what is perhaps the most significant set of events in the history of western North America. These treaties established a framework of interaction between Natives and non-Natives which persists to this day. Each party understood the relationship between humans and the land in fundamentally different ways. As a result, the treaties meant—and continue to mean—very different things to First Nations and to the dominant society.

Between 1870 and 1908, the Government of Canada signed a series of eight treaties with the First Peoples of Manitoba and Saskatchewan and Alberta (or the North-West Territories, as they were then known). The seventh of these (Treaty 7) was signed with the Siksika (Blackfoot), Kainai (Blood), Peigan, Tsuu T'ina (Sarcee), and Stoney people at Blackfoot Crossing, on the Bow River, in Alberta, in 1877. The report of the government negotiator, Lieutenant-

Indian Wars service medal

Glenbow Museum

United States Army servicemen who saw duty during the conflict
with the Lakota in the Western Plains received medals like this.

Pipe tomahawk

Glenbow Museum (AF 435)

Pipe tomahawks were presented to Native leaders by Euro-Canadian and Euro-American traders. They functioned neither as weapons nor as pipes, but indicated prestige. This one was owned by the Siksika Only Owl.

Presidential inauguration medals

Glenbow Museum (R5.454 and R5.471)

Presidential inauguration medals were presented by the United States
government to tribal leaders. These medals commemorate the
inauguration of James Buchanan in 1857 and Benjamin Harrison
in 1889.

Governor and Special Indian Commissioner David Laird, reflects an agreeable process in which the leaders of the First Nations acknowledged the economic plight facing their people and sought the help and protectionof the federal government.[2] Laird and the government believed that, in exchange for this assistance, the people surrendered all rights to their land except the relatively small areas set aside for Reserves. Not surprisingly, the First Nations' perspectives of these events are quite different.

Connections

The unwillingness, or even the inability, of the First Peoples to relinquish title to the land reflects their close ties to it. The First Nations and the Euro-Canadians had, and continue to have, fundamentally different understandings of the place of human beings within the universe. Judeo-Christian theology explains that the Creator made humans in His image and gave them jurisdiction over all of creation.

The Blackfoot people understand the world very differently.[3] They are Nitsitapi, or the Real People, and are part of an integrated world with the Above People (Sspomitapiikski), the On Earth People (Ksaahkommitapiiksi) and the Underwater People (Sooyiitapiiksi). While humans were given intellect as a special power, other beings also possess unique gifts and the balance of these gifts or powers creates an equality among all animate beings. To the Blackfoot people, almost everything is animate:

The world view of Blackfoot people consists of probably five or six important concepts. Number one is what we would refer to as constant motion or constant flux. This constant motion is an observation of human beings, in this case Blackfoot people, of what's going on on the earth and also what's going on at the cosmic or universe level. Things are forever moving; things are forever changing. However, observations lead to some notice of some regular patterns and those regular patterns are things like the seasons of the year, things like migrations of animals and birds. Those are examples of regular patterns.

Out of this constant flux (because everything is moving) arises the fact that human beings and everything in the universe consist as energy force. In many cases Native people would refer to it as spirit. As a consequence, since everything is spirit or made of energy forces, then the next step is: everything is animate. There is hardly anything in Blackfoot that we could refer to as inanimate. Now, if everything is animate, and if you combine it with this notion of constant change, this constant flux occurring, then you begin to come up with this concept of relationships. Everything is interrelated. So that I'm related not only to my immediate family; not only to other human beings. I'm also related to the rest of creation. I'm related to the trees, the rocks, other animals. All those things are full of energy. They are energy forces too. So, they are *all my relations.*[4]

The idea of one's place or one's territory also has different overtones for the Blackfoot people than it does for Euro-Canadians. For the latter, territory can easily be seen as the space within which one's resources are held. It is also a place where one lives. For the Blackfoot, southern Alberta is this and much more. Their territory includes the places where the connections with their relations among the other beings were first made. Access to and maintenance of these places is important for the continuation of their cultural identity.

Blackfoot people would say, "If you go out of Blackfoot territory, make sure that you are very respectful of what is going on outside of Blackfoot territory. You're safe on the inside, but you're

Treaty medal

Glenbow Museum (R5.405)

In the Canadian West, medals were presented to chiefs, sub-chiefs and headmen at the signing of the treaties. This medal commemorates Treaty 7, the 1877 agreement between the Siksika, Blood, Peigan, Tsuu T'ina and Stoney people and the government of Canada.

Red Crow, Head Chief of the Bloods (1892)

Glenbow Archives (NA-668-53)

Red Crow is wearing a chief's uniform given to him as part of the
treaty payments. Around his neck is a Treaty 7 medal and on his right
breast is a medal presented to him when he visited Brantford,
Ontario, in 1886.

not safe on the outside." Why? Well because we know in Blackfoot territory what the relational network is because we've been observing it. We know how to relate to the animals; we know how to relate to the ecosystem and so forth. But outside Blackfoot territory, you don't know.[5]

The Blackfoot made considerable efforts to demarcate their territory—this space within which they could maintain their vital connections to the land and, thereby, to their relations. At several places in southern Alberta there are large boulder outlines of a male figure. These are effigies of Napi, a creator-trickster figure in Blackfoot culture, and the sites are called "Where Napi Lay Down." The Siksika performed ceremonies at these locations to protect themselves against trespassers from other First Nations. Reg Crow Shoe, a Peigan cere-monialist, describes how this ceremony worked:

They put sweetgrass on the ground and made a human effigy of Napi so the other tribes would not come through because the Blackfoot claimed this part of the territory. The sweetgrass rep-resented the other Native people and the rocks held them down at that spot. And should they cross that particular spot into our territory, and we encountered them in battle, we would only be dealing with the physical existence; the spiritual existence stayed back at the point where they crossed this abstract border.[6]

The importance of maintaining the integrity of their territory is reflected in the meetings undertaken by members of the Blackfoot confederacy prior to the meetings with the govern-ment representatives. In 1875, two years before the formal treaty negotiations, the leaders of the Siksika, Kainai and Peigan met to map out their strategy. These discussions were recorded by Jean L'Hereux, a non-Native who represented himself as a priest and who traveled with these people. Historian Walter Hildebrandt outlines the major points which the Blackfoot wished to discuss with the government:

The two major items really on this list were the fact that they wanted the Cree and Metis to be kept off their lands, because the Cree and Metis were hunting a lot of buffalo. The Blackfoot Con-federacy was really quite dismayed by the consequences of their agreement to keep peace after the Mounties arrived. Keeping the peace meant that they could no longer militarily protect their terri-tory. What happened was that the Metis and the Cree began, with some temerity, to just go into their territory and hunt the buffalo.

A second item was a really overt statement that the Blackfoot Confederacy would like more to be done to protect the buffalo.[7]

Neither of these items was addressed in the written treaty. When Button Chief of the Kainai brought the matter up during the negotiations, Laird replied that federal legislation which had been passed to limit buffalo hunting would protect the herds. However, Cree and Metis, as Canadian citizens, could only be prohibited from entering Blackfoot Reserve lands. The rest of the territory was open to whomever wished to cross it. Access to Blackfoot sacred geography was being compromised and their relational networks were being disrupted.

The loss of a way of life, the dislocation from important spiritual places, and living within an unfamiliar social structure imposed by the Reserve system all contributed to the cultural collapse of many First Nations. The relational network with the rest of creation seemed to have been shattered. This disintegration was abetted by government policies which offered two alternatives for First Peoples: assimilation or extinction.

Siksika Ok'an (Sundance) camp at Blackfoot Crossing
on the Bow River (ca. 1920)
Glenbow Archives (NA-331-1)

Persistent Voices

Still, the First Nations cultures have persisted and today there is a promise of cultural renewal. A key element in this renewal is a reinforced sense of place and a connection with the land. Many First Nations people have moved to urban centers where they strive to maintain or even renew the connections with the non-human world. Often, making these connections requires ceremonies which may not easily be undertaken within a city. This leads to a perplexing contradiction for First Nations youth:

A lot of kids here [in Calgary] are told, by a lot of the elders and traditionalists, they're told to hang on to their culture. They're told to go to their elders when they need guidance. It's very difficult sometimes for kids that are far away from their home to talk to their elders. It's very hard for these kids sometimes to even know where they come from. Maybe they've been living in the urban environment all their life. What do we do for those kids? What do we do for kids that see the sidewalk—that's their earth? So I started listening to the kids. And I heard their stories and I listened to their disappointment in us as adults. I heard their anger about things that are told to them that they should do when there's no way they can do it.

But what happens when they start wanting to make the connections that they start to learn about? They start learning about sweats. They start learning about sundances. And they say, "Well, I want to do this." There's no place here to do that. It would be really nice if there was a place— I see bush around the city—a place just for us. Where we could go, set up, do all the things we need to do.[8]

Rosa John tries to find other ways for people living in the city to make the connections with the land. She believes that it is key for people to find life wherever they live:

People talk about earth as if it's only dirt, the dirt that we have to attach ourselves to. But earth can also mean that sidewalk, those telephone poles, those big buildings. And what we talk about with the kids when we're gathering is that the attachment to earth is all about respect. It all means that—not just respect for when you go in the bush. But respect for where you're living, because that's earth too. We're taught that everything is alive. You have to think of that sidewalk as having life. You have to think of those buildings—they have a life too. If we see ourselves in that position maybe it would be easier to have that respect.[9]

The connection with the land and the establishment of a relationship with the rest of creation can be important in creating positive self-images for First Nations people.

Some of the people who are most in need of finding a positive image and understanding the traditional teachings which provide this reinforcement are the First Nations inmates of Canada's prisons. While aboriginal people comprise less than four percent of Canada's population, they represent almost fourteen percent of the prison population. For many inmates, the social conditions in which they grew up eroded their self-esteem and convinced them that they would inevitably fail.[10] For others, crime is a way of striking back at the dominant society and salvaging their pride and self-respect.[11]

Most programs developed by Corrections Canada contribute little to the rehabilitation of First Nations inmates, since they do not take into account the physical, social or cultural environment into which First Nations inmates return upon their release. These attitudes by the prison officials began to change in the early 1980s, when Native inmates began protesting for the right to conduct ceremonies within prison. Their demands were supported by Native and non-Native criminologists, psychologists, jurists and elders who recognized the potential value of these ceremonies. Dan Beatty Paywiss is an inmate at the Drumheller Medium Security Penitentiary:

We had our first sweat lodge here in Drumheller in 1984. And at the same time there was a big change going on within the institution, I noticed a big change within myself. I guess one of the most common problems of prisoners everywhere is that we suffer from a lack of self-esteem. Our spirituality and our elders give us that opportunity to discard that. There's no need to feel bad for being a Native person.[12]

These ceremonies have also changed the prison as a whole:

When sweat lodges first came here in 1984 we had a problem with drug abuse, serious drug abuse—sniffing—and there was racial problems and tensions. And all that started disappearing. It's still here, but guys started getting a better understanding of what harmony is.[13]

The struggle remains, however, for inmates to maintain their spirituality and connections with the land when they are released. Indeed, many First Nations people are struggling to keep their traditions. Bruce Starlight of the Tsuu T'ina Nation finds that modern technology is overpowering his culture:

It is the tools of your culture that is destroying our culture. Because there is no need to get on the land, you know, even to take a walk. There's no need because you've got the fax, you've got a telephone, you've got tv. So the conveniences of your culture is what is destroying our culture. We find that we have to drag our kids to the land, kicking and screaming. They won't come out just to be on the land. So we have to encourage them or entice them to come out to the land. And that could happen anywhere. Even in isolated areas you have your satellites. White culture, every day.[14]

It is difficult to maintain traditional relationships in the face of constant pressure from an ever-expanding technological society.

Museums can play a vital role in First Nations' cultural renewal. Many of the objects in museum collections played an important role in maintaining connections between human beings and the rest of Creation. Other objects carry with them memories of historical events and the people who experienced those times. In some cases, these were important leaders and spokesmen; in other cases they are people's grandmothers and grandfathers. Access to these objects can help rebuild relationships which have been disrupted and restore cultural memories which may be on the brink of being forgotten.

Such access can also enhance the institutions. As these cultural connections are shared with museum staff, the museum may become more aware of the significance which objects have for people and of the multilayered meaning carried by items from non-Western cultures. Communicating these meanings to wider audiences will lead to greater cultural awareness and understanding. No museum can hope to do more than this.

1. See, for instance, William H. Truettner (ed.), *The West as America: Reinterpreting Images of the Frontier, 1820–1920* (Washington, DC: Smithsonian Institution Press, 1991).

2. Alexander Morris, *The Treaties of Canada with the Indians of Manitoba and the North-West Territories* (1880; rpt, Saskatoon: Fifth House, 1991).

3. The term "Blackfoot" includes Kainai (Blood), Siksika and Peigan nations.

4. The quotes in this paper are taken from interviews conducted by the authors. Interview with Leroy Little Bear, December 16, 1995. Leroy Little Bear, a Kainai, is a professor of aboriginal law at the University of Lethbridge. The interview is on file at the Glenbow Museum.

We wish to thank the following for their discussions, hospitality, and insights: the late Dan Weasel Moccasin, Sr.; Daniel and Rosaline Weasel Moccasin; Florence Scout; Joe and Josephine Crow Shoe; Reg and Rose Crow Shoe; Pat Provost; Jenny Bruisedhead; Morris Little Wolf; Beverly and Adolph Hungry Wolf; Paul Raczka. Daphne Baine of CKUA Radio co-produced the series "Voices from the Land" and offered support and advice on the interviews. Our research has been generously supported by the Glenbow.

5. Interview with Leroy Little Bear, December 16, 1995. On file at the Glenbow Museum.

6. Interview with Reg Crow Shoe, November 2, 1995. Reg Crow Shoe is a Peigan ceremonialist and Director of the Keep Our Circle Strong Cultural Centre on the Peigan Reserve. The interview is on file at the Glenbow Museum.

7. Interview with Walter Hildebrandt, May 21, 1996. Walter Hilderbrandt is an historian and researcher for the Treaty 7 Tribal Council's project "The True Spirit and Intent of Treaty 7." The interview is on file at the Glenbow Museum.

8. Interview with Rosa John, May 2, 1996. Rosa John is part Taino and part Black. She and her husband, Melvin John, are involved with Native theatre and Native youth projects in Calgary. The interview is on file at the Glenbow Museum.

9. Interview with Rosa John, May 2, 1996.

10. Interview with Dan Beatty Paywiss, May 19, 1996. Dan Beatty Paywiss is an Ojibwa from Ontario. He has been an inmate of Canada's prisons for the past fourteen years and is Vice Chief of the Indian Brotherhood at the Drumheller Medium Security Prison. The interview is on file at the Glenbow Museum.

11. Interview with Wayne Stonechild, May 19, 1996. Wayne Stonechild is Cree and Chief of the Indian Brotherhood at the Drumheller Medium Security Prison. The interview is on file at the Glenbow Museum.

12. Interview with Dan Beatty Paywiss, May 19, 1996.

13. Interview with Dan Beatty Paywiss, May 19, 1996.

14. Interview with Bruce Starlight, May 9, 1996. Bruce Starlight is a Tsuu T'ina ceremonialist and is a student in the Department of Linguistics at the University of Calgary. The interview is on file at the Glenbow Museum.

Illusions and Deceptions
The Indian in Popular Culture

JAMES H. NOTTAGE

 OR THE MOST PART, THE WHITE MAN'S VISUAL EXPRESSIONS OF NATIVE
peoples have been dominant. Those expressions are pervasive and have appeared in all media
throughout the past five centuries. Such is true of the manner in which the first nations of
Canada have been treated and perceived, and such is true for the manner in which the
American Indian has been viewed. In no less painterly a fashion than that of the visual artist,
the creators of literature, theater, film, television, advertising and marketing have manufac-
tured and maintained stereotypes. In the process these components of popular culture have
helped to erase individual and cultural identities of the Indian. Consequently, images of the
feathered headdress, the tomahawk and related conventions have helped to assure everyone
that all Indians are the same.

Robert F. Berkhofer reminds us that "for most whites . . . the Indian of imagination and
ideology has been as real, perhaps more real, than the Native American of actual existence
and contact. As preconception became conception and conception became fact, the Indian
was used for the ends of argument, art, and entertainment."[1] Assuredly, many portrayals of
the Indian are absurd, but they are never trivial. Even positive stereotypes are not assurances
of innocence, but often express the dominant culture's attitude towards the Indian. The
ways that stereotypes of the Indian condition the behavior of the broader culture, even
subconsciously, is a profound reason for investigating the impact of popular culture.

It is disappointing that in some institutions the collecting of items of kitsch, of popular
culture, is considered beneath the dignity of their collections, even though such items are
profound cultural indicators. Granted, salt and pepper shakers, sports team pennants, advertising gadgets and other items in the shape of the Indian warrior or princess might not be as
significant aesthetically or economically as a fine painting or sculpture. They do, however,
convey powerful messages about the culture which produced them. They do not convey images of Indians themselves, but rather images of attitudes—bias both positive and negative.

Perhaps they are not as respectable as fine arts in part because they are largely from our
own time. That, however, is not entirely true. Hair combs in the shape of Indians, the ubiquitous cigar store Indian, illustrative engravings and other materials date back to before the

Flatware (1894–1896)

Tiffany and Company

11 × 3 in. and 9 × 2 in.; Autry Museum of Western Heritage

Exhibited at the Chicago World's Fair in 1893, this pattern of silver
was based upon elements taken from George Catlin's drawings. The
addition of other stylistic "Indian" designs completed the package.
These examples are part of a set which belonged to William
Randolph Hearst.

eighteenth century. More important, perhaps they are less respectable because they are more difficult to take seriously. Somehow even those less perceptive can see the commercial qualities of everything from Indian motorcycles to Big Chief tablets. Maybe a part of the problem is that we have become too comfortable with the commercial exploitation of the Indian image.[2]

At the Philadelphia Exposition in 1876 the nation celebrated its first hundred years in the midst of failed Indian policy. News of the death of George Custer and his men at the Little Bighorn greeted fair goers that year while at the same time the Gillander Company exhibited its "Pioneer" glassware, which also became known as "Westward Ho." With lids topped with kneeling scalp-locked warriors and other emblazoned imagery of the frontier, this inexpensive product line became quite popular. At the Chicago World's Fair in 1893, Tiffany and Company proudly exhibited an extraordinary and expensive line of flatware with finials on sterling silver spoons, forks and knives in the shape of Indian warriors. The designs were taken directly from George Catlin's 1830s drawings. They were exclusive because of cost and were purchased by the likes of William Randolph Hearst, who had a large set. Others have commented about the manner in which the Indian was displayed at the Chicago exposition. Indians themselves were used to demonstrate their "quaint" ways of life; even William F. "Buffalo Bill" Cody performed in Chicago, bringing with him Plains Indians who had participated in the wars and lent an aura of authenticity to his fanciful portrayal of the conquest of the frontier and of the Indian. As displayed at the fairs the Indian was meant to reinforce the white man's perceptions of him.[3]

In performance the Indian has been a part of our lives through theater, Wild West shows, film and television since the late nineteenth century. Buffalo Bill Cody was the perfect carrier of interest in the Indian. He even made movies, one a "history" of the Indian wars, another his own biography filled with Indian fighting. From the very beginning of the silent era to *Dances with Wolves*, movies have been imbued with the latest ideas about how sympathetically the Indian should be treated. In fact, people today are surprised to know that Indians themselves objected to film portrayals from the very beginning. Richard V. Spencer, in *The Moving Picture World*, on March 18, 1911, wrote that "the reservation Indians of the West and Northwest are registering strenuous objections with the Indian Bureau at Washington regarding the portrayal of Indian life in the films. President Taft has been appealed to and urged to help the redmen in their fight against the moving picture theaters and the alleged misrepresentation of Indian life as shown in the moving picture films. Indian Commissioner Robert G. Valentine has also been displeased by the popular Indian pictures and has promised to aid the Indians in every way possible to eliminate the objectionable features of Indian life portrayals. Delegations from the Shoshone, Cheyenne and Arapaho reservations have gone to Washington to take the matter up with the government authorities."

Twenty years later a small article, hidden near the back page of the *Hollywood Citizen News*, on June 6, 1932 reported that "250 American Indians held a pow-wow . . . in protest against Negroes and Mexicans representing themselves as Indians in motion picture work." The article recounted that "the Indians, representing 18 different tribes, assailed the practice, under the leadership of Jim Thorpe, famous one-time athlete. All signed a register which Thorpe will use to gain co-operation of casting bureaus in a plan to check the identity of those who apply for film jobs as Indians."

Since the earliest days of silent films, Native Americans have been portrayed by both

Umbrella (ca. 1905)

Carved ivory; 30 × 3 in.; Autry Museum of Western Heritage

Oral tradition suggests that this umbrella was a gift of state from an American diplomat to a European dignitary. In any case, the carved ivory images of the Indian are one more example of the Indian as a symbol of America.

Picture puzzle: Native Americans and the Singer (1906)

Singer Sewing Machine Company

8 × 10 in.; Autry Museum of Western Heritage

This early use of the term "Native American" is significant. Photographs taken in Montana in this period show native peoples with sewing machines, demonstrating that they were consumers as well as advertising devices.

F. O. C. DARLEY (1822–1888)
An Indian Raid (1860s)
Pencil, ink and wash on paper; 17½ × 23½ in.
Autry Museum of Western Heritage

Darley illustrated the works of James Fenimore Cooper and created
many such illustrations even though he never visited the West. This
example was created as a design for decorating Union script.

non-Indians and real Indians. Film has also been consumed by both groups. Film became such a pervasive part of life that cheering audiences would pay their dimes and nickels to watch even the poorest of low-budget Westerns. James Welch describes cheering in the theater as the cavalry comes to the rescue, defeating the Indians in films shown in Browning, Montana, in the 1940s and 1950s. At the end, when the lights are turned up in the theater, he reveals that the audience was made up of Indians. He writes, "In those days not many Indians cared that they were rooting against themselves. The Indians in the film had been portrayed as the very embodiment of evil, and Hollywood had staked its existence on the notion that whipping the forces of evil (Indians) made people feel good, even Indians, who would pay their money and eat their popcorn in anticipation of the happy ending, and when it came it was like the satisfaction of whipping the boys in the next town in basketball." Take the shirt off Tonto, and you will see a real Indian such as Jay Silverheels in the 1950s or Michael Horse in the 1980s. It was all role playing, in front of the camera or in front of the theater screen.[4]

Of course, there have been many forms of Indian plays and playing Indian. Children have played Indian for generations either at home or in the forms which have been promoted by the Boy Scouts, Girl Scouts, Indian guide groups and other organizations and clubs.[5] In the same manner, adults have participated in fraternal and social organizations which utilize Indian names, imagery, clothing and other "native" elements in their programs. The Fraternal Order of Red Men utilized Indian names and imagery in its activities in the late nineteenth century and members dressed up in leather suits with feathered headdresses and painted their faces. New Age practitioners today do not step too far away from such caricatures to promote their idealized images of the Indian as child and defender of nature and mimic him with their preconceived ideas of what it means to be Indian. Worse are others who have taken playing Indian to extremes far beyond this—those hobbyists who slavishly reproduce nineteenth-century Indian costume, school themselves in every nuance of Indian history and culture and then dress-up to become Indian. These Indian "wannabes" may be the ultimate insult to native peoples who now are told in effect that anyone can actually be an Indian if they just do their homework and "get it right." You can as well if you get an outfit too.

Theater, radio, Wild West shows, film, television, toys and other products have been used as canvases to express the ideas of studios, authors, actors, and designers and manufacturers. They have been created to appeal to targeted audiences, reflecting both popular opinion and attitude. If you remove the makeup of the theater, you may see the imposter playing the Indian. You might see something of yourself. Objects of popular culture are shaped and colored by a veil of varying density, woven with threads of bias and assumptions about audiences and consumers. Ignorance allows older attitudes to be repeated. It is not enough that James Earle Fraser's sculptural masterpiece *End of the Trail* might be viewed as the fine art that it is. The work has been repeated in every form imaginable. In Cecil B. DeMille's *Union Pacific* in 1939 an image of it is part of an introductory slide. Even today it can be seen in Indian-made beaded belt buckles, factory-made woven rugs and no end of other products. Lo, the poor Indian!

Some of the most powerful and inciteful statements about the impact of popular images of the Indian have come from Indian commentators. In 1992 the Woodland Cultural Centre in Brantford, Ontario, produced a traveling exhibition and accompanying catalogue titled *Fluffs and Feathers: An Exhibit on the Symbols of Indianness.* Joanna Bedard, executive director of the Centre, commented about how important it is for a society to choose its own

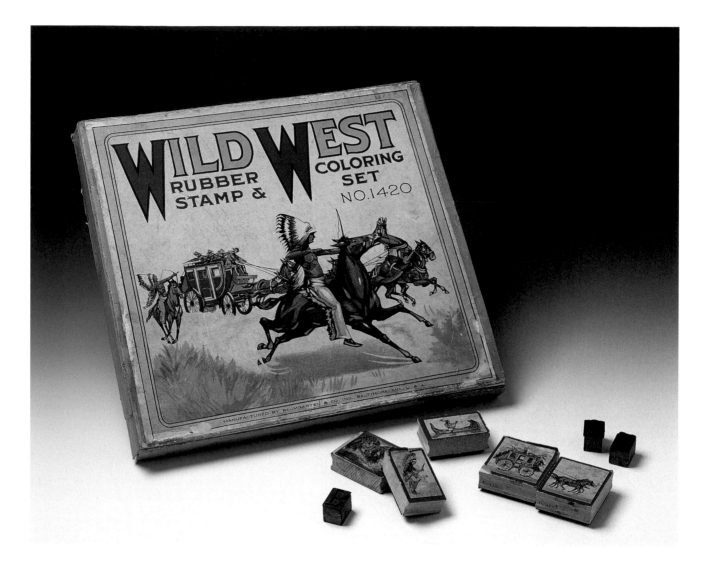

Rubber stamp coloring set (1890s)

Baumgarten & Co., Baltimore

Box: 10 × 10 in.; Autry Museum of Western Heritage

By the 1890s, the influence of Buffalo Bill Cody's Wild West show was
evident in the design of toys, board games and other products.

symbols as "a way of empowering itself." She went further, writing, "What then happens to a culture whose symbols are chosen by outsiders, by those who do not understand its deepest beliefs, structures and ways of life? What kind of interpretation of a society can come from symbols designed not to elevate conscious understanding to the highest of that society's ideas but to reduce that understanding to categories which debase or ridicule? The opposite of empowering occurs. Feelings of rage, impotence and powerlessness are evoked. The symbols are not representations but caricatures."[6]

Therefore, all-Indian schools in Oklahoma and elsewhere thrive with their own symbols and mascots with Indian names and images. Therefore, non-Indians are confounded when they learn that their visions of the Atlanta Braves baseball team and its "tomahawk chop" are offensive to Indians themselves. What makes you think of Indians? Are your visions of eagle feathers, tomahawks, tipis, totem poles, fringed buckskins and moccasins truly reflective of Indian people? Does the presence of these symbols in everyday objects really tell you anything about real Indian people? Or do they tell you about yourself?

1. Robert F. Berkhofer, *The White Man's Indian: Images of the American Indian from Columbus to the Present* (New York: Alfred A. Knopf, 1978), pp. 96–100.

2. Useful studies for the comprehension of the popular image of the Indian include: Raymond William Stedman, *Shadows of the Indian: Stereotypes in American Culture* (Norman: University of Oklahoma Press, 1967); Brian W. Dippie, *The Vanishing American: White Attitudes and U.S. Indian Policy* (Lawrence: University Press of Kansas, 1982); and Berkhofer, *The White Man's Indian*.

3. See J. C. H. King, "A Century of Indian Shows: Canadian and United States Exhibitions in London 1825–1925," *Native American Studies*, Vol. 5, No. 1, 1991; Robert W. Rydell, *All the World's a Fair: Visions of Empire at American International Expositions, 1876–1916* (Chicago: The University of Chicago Press, 1987); Phyllis Rogers, "Buffalo Bill's Wild West, The Image of the American Indian Produced and Directed by 'Buffalo Bill,'" UCLA Museum of Cultural History Pamphlet Series Number 13, 1981; Richard White and Patricia Limerick, *The Frontier in American Culture* (Berkeley: University of California Press, 1994); L. G. Moses, *Wild West Shows and the Images of American Indians, 1882–1933* (Albuquerque: University of New Mexico Press, 1966).

4. See James Welch, *Killing Custer: The Battle of the Little Bighorn and the Fate of the Plains Indians* (New York: W. W. Norton & Company, 1994); for general references to film and the Indian see also Gretchen M. Bataille and Charles L.P. Silet, eds., *The Pretend Indians: Images of Native Americans in the Movies* (Ames: Iowa State University Press, 1980); John A. Price, "The Stereotyping of North American Indians in Motion Pictures," *Ethnohistory*, Vol. 20, No. 2, Spring 1973; Michael Hilger, *The American Indian in Film* (Metuchen, NJ: Scarecrow Press, 1986); and *The Kaleidoscopic Lens: How Hollywood Views Ethnic Groups*, ed. Randall M. Miller (Englewood Cliffs, NJ: Ozer, 1980).

5. Arlene B. Hirschfelder, *American Indian Stereotypes in the World of Children: A Reader and Bibliography* (Metuchen, NJ: Scarecrow Press, 1982); and Brenda Berkman, "The Vanishing Race: Conflicting Images of the American in Children's Literature, 1880–1930," *North Dakota Quarterly*, Spring 1976, pp. 31–40.

6. Deborah Doxtator, *Fluffs and Feathers: An Exhibit on the Symbols of Indianness* (Brantford, Ont.: Woodland Cultural Centre, 1992), p. 5.

An American (ca. 1893)

A. Hoen & Co., Baltimore

38½ × 27½ in.; Buffalo Bill Historical Center,

Gift of The Coe Foundation

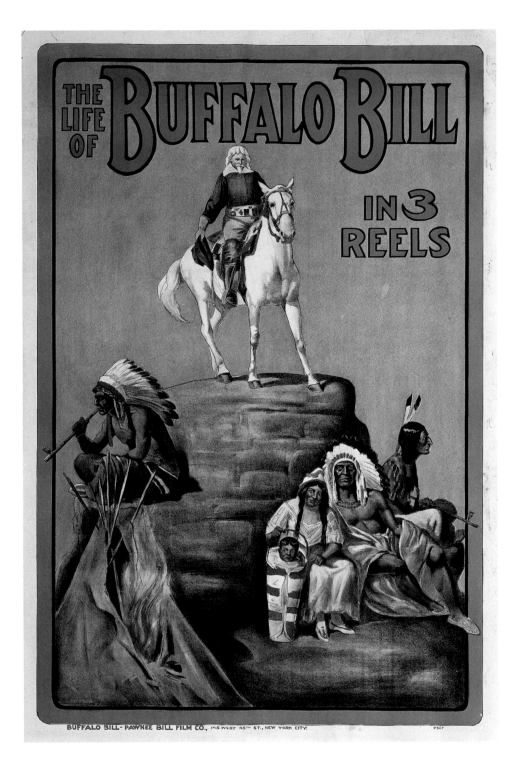

Film poster: The Life of Buffalo Bill (1910)

Buffalo Bill–Pawnee Bill Film Company

48 × 34 in.; Autry Museum of Western Heritage

William F. Cody showed Indians to the world on stage and in film.
Re-enactments of the Custer battle and portrayal of Cody as the
ultimate avenger of Custer helped to ingrain stereotypes even though
Cody consistently employed real Indians in his productions.

Fruit crate labels
Prairie Bell, *Sierra Vista Packing Company,* **Indian Belle**, *Boydston Brothers, 11 × 11 in. each; Autry Museum of Western Heritage*

Stereotypes of the Indian maiden and warbonnet-dressed warrior became common conventions on such labels in the years prior to World War II. Such images often bear striking resemblance to those in films of the time.

Trade Sign (1930s)

Calumet Baking Powder Company

H 24 × W 16 × D 2 in.; Autry Museum of Western Heritage

The familiar Calumet baking powder cans with their image of the
Indian were marketed in store displays with these wooden carvings.

Neon sign (1960s)

H 31 × W 33 × D 9 in.; Autry Museum of Western Heritage

Stereotypes of the Indian have appeared in many forms of signage
and architecture. This example from a 1960s cafe is typical.

Trade sign (1940s)

Pontiac Automobiles

H 43 × W 53 × D 1 in.; Autry Museum of Western Heritage

This weather vane is typical of those used to decorate car dealerships throughout the country. The image of the Indian became a generic one, a familiar silhouette used to represent Pontiac cars.

Weller Pottery Souevo vase (left) (1900–1917)

8³⁄₄ × 6¹⁄₄ in.

Pueblo tourist vase (right) (1970s)

D 4 in.; Autry Museum of Western Heritage

Images of the Indian and design motifs taken from native arts
became popular elements in the arts and crafts movement, especially
in pottery by Weller and Rookwood. Traditional Indian pottery was
collected and used decoratively as well. Unsophisticated tourist
demands for Indian pottery ultimately cheapened some of their work.

Hopi gourd rattle (ca. 1990)

H 12 × W 9 × D 7 in.; Autry Museum of Western Heritage

Evidence of popular culture within Indian culture has been made
manifest in many ways.

Hopi kachina (1987)

National Cowboy Hall of Fame and Western Heritage Center

H 3 in.; Gift of Make a Wish Foundation

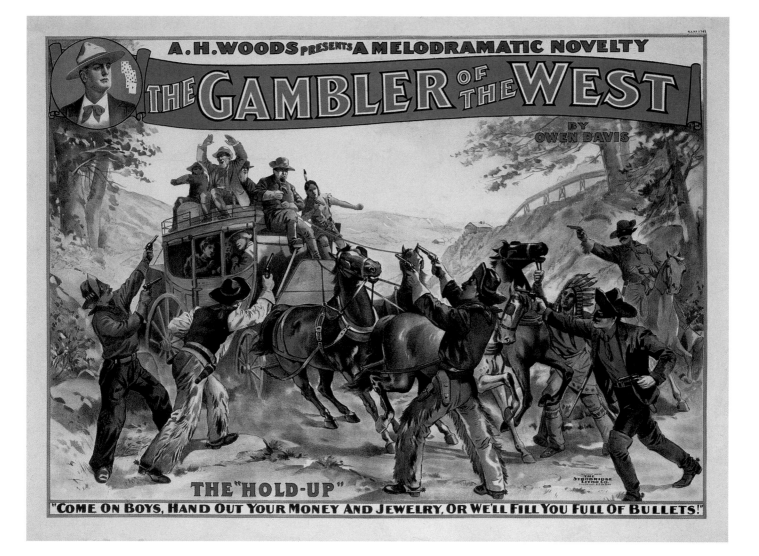

Melodrama poster: The Gambler of the West (1906)

32 × 46 in.; Autry Museum of Western Heritage

It is common to see Indians portrayed as villains on stage.
This example is unusual in showing Indians as both attackers
and defenders.

93

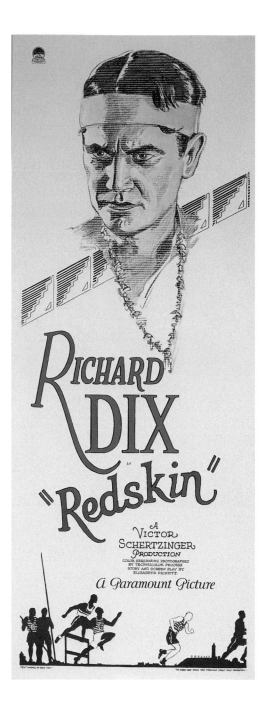

Insert poster: "Redskin" (1929)

Paramount

40 × 18 in.; Autry Museum of Western Heritage

Film poster: With General Custer at the Little Big Horn (1926)

Sunset Pictures

46 × 32 in.; Autry Museum of Western Heritage

The Custer story has been played out in a huge number of films
which have tended to reflect the level of social conscience at the time
of their production. This example clearly shows the Indian as enemy,
contrasted with productions such as *Little Big Man*, which conveyed
an opposite point of view.

95

Lobby card: The Vanishing American (1926)

Paramount

12½ × 15½ in.; Autry Museum of Western Heritage

Based upon the writing of Zane Grey, this film, starring a white actor,
conveyed the sense of 1926 sympathy for the Indian.

96

JOE DEYONG

Costume design, possibly for Union Pacific (ca. 1939)

Watercolor on board; 27 × 21 in.; Autry Museum of Western Heritage

DeYong was Charles M. Russell's protégé and came to Hollywood where he created costume designs for Cecil B. DeMille and other producers. His practical knowledge of Indian history added to illusions of authenticity on film.

Headdress and shirt

Shirt: H 40 × W 21 × D 9 in., Headdress: W 12 × D 19 in.
Autry Museum of Western Heritage

Worn in film by John Sitting Bull, the adopted son of Chief Sitting
Bull. John Sitting Bull appeared in Western films as late as the 1950s.
The use of real Indians in their own garb was often meant to convey
a sense of authenticity in films—just as Buffalo Bill Cody used John
Sitting Bull's fellow Lakota in his Wild West show.

War bonnet (ca. 1950s)
H 26 × W 28 × L 20 in.
National Cowboy Hall of Fame and Western Heritage Center
Gift of Iron Eyes Cody

Iron Eyes Cody performed in Western films beginning in the 1920s
and lasting into the 1980s. He provided Indian objects, including this
headdress, for use in film. Ultimately, he became an icon himself and
reinforced ideas of the Indian as child and protector of nature when
he appeared in "Keep America Beautiful" campaigns, posing as the
Indian with the tear rolling down his face.

Lobby card: Broken Arrow (1950)

20th Century-Fox

12½ × 15½ in.; Autry Museum of Western Heritage

Hailed as a strongly pro-Indian production, *Broken Arrow* still
featured non-Indians in Indian roles and offered nothing new
compared with sympathetic portrayals from the silent film era.

Lobby card: Chief Crazy Horse (1955)

Universal-International Picture Company

15½ × 12½ in.; Autry Museum of Western Heritage

Non-Indians commonly played Indian roles in film.
Some examples are more obvious than others.

101

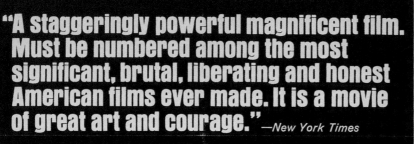

Film poster: Soldier Blue (1970)

Avco-Embassy

46 × 32 in.; Autry Museum of Western Heritage

Violent and strongly anti-government, *Soldier Blue* grew from
sentiments of the anti-Vietnam era.

Film poster: Dances With Wolves (1990)

Majestic Films International, German Release

45 ¾ × 32 ¼ in.; Autry Museum of Western Heritage

Environmentally and socially conscious, *Dances with Wolves* gained
worldwide popularity for its expressions of respect and sympathy for
the Indian—even though its own forms of historical manipulation
and stereotyping have been described as serious faults.

103

KATHY SMITH, DESIGNER
Dress: Son of the Morning Star (1991)
H 56 × W 19 × D 9 in.
Autry Museum of Western Heritage, donated by Republic Pictures

Smith made important contributions to the realistic portrayal of
Plains Indians in this made-for-television production and for *Dances
With Wolves.* She has studied historical narratives and the paintings
of Karl Bodmer and George Catlin.

Jacket

Order of Red Men

H 32 × W 21 × D 9 in.; Autry Museum of Western Heritage

105

Play suit and box (1930s)
Wornova Play Clothes
Box: H 14 × W 12 × D 1¾ in., Play suit with headdress:
48 in. H overall; Autry Museum of Western Heritage

From homemade versions to mass-produced products, there have
long been toys available to fulfill the fantasy needs of play. Such
products almost always reflect engrained stereotypes of what it has
been thought Indians should look like.

106

Boxed figure, Aurora (1970s)

H 10½ × W 7 in. × D 2½ in.

Squirt gun (1950s)

H 5¼ × W 2½ × D 3 in.

Mattel cap gun (1960s)

H 12½ × W 13 × D 2 in.

Autry Museum of Western Heritage

Television Westerns generated a variety of products tied to programs
and their main characters. Sometimes a product was repackaged to
sell to several markets such as the cap gun shown here which has
grips from an African themed product. It became Indian with the
addition of stylized symbols and images.

NUDIE THE RODEO TAILOR
Suede shirt (ca. 1958)
Tonto poster
Wheaties cereal premium; 77¼ × 17¼ in.
Autry Museum of Western Heritage

Cereal box tops made it possible for children in the 1950s to acquire
posters of the Lone Ranger and Tonto. The suede shirt was worn
by Jay Silverheels in his role as Tonto in the Lone Ranger television
series. Jay Silverheels, of Mohawk heritage, was one of a long line of
performers to play the Tonto role. All the actors who played the role
from the 1930s to the 1980s were American Indian.

Silk Shirt (1930s)
Rodeo Ben, Philadelphia
Autry Museum of Western Heritage,
donated by Mr. and Mrs. Gene Autry

Indian imagery in clothing during the twentieth century has been both realistic and stylistic. This example was used in stage performances by Gene Autry. Other examples with embroidery by Nudie, the Hollywood tailor, were worn by country-Western performers and parade equestrians throughout the century.

Custer Died for Your Sins
$4\frac{1}{2} \times 6\frac{1}{2}$ in.
Century of Dishonor
7×9 in.
Dime novels
8×10 in.
Pulp novels
7×9 in.
Autry Museum of Western Heritage

Native American Artists— Expressing Their Own Identity

MIKE LESLIE

*N*O OTHER RACE IN AMERICA IS CONFRONTED BY SUCH UNRELENTING stereotyping as Native Americans. The relationship between native people and white America is fraught with dichotomy. The dominant culture molds, reshapes and packages the portrait of native people to whatever image best suits its needs at any given time. As essayist and critic Paul Chaat Smith poignantly observes,

The country can't make up its mind. One decade we're invisible, another dangerous. Obsolete and quaint, a rather boring people suitable for schoolkids and family vacations, then suddenly we're cool and mysterious . . . some now regard us as keepers of planetary secrets and the only salvation for a world bent on destroying itself. Heck, we're just plain folk, but no one wants to hear that.[1]

Adding to this bewildering environment is the emergence of an active contemporary Native American fine art movement.

All artists contend with obstacles and intrusions, for artistic expression more often than not evokes a subjective response from the viewer. For many native artists, however, arbitrary restrictions and evaluations stem more from racially preconceived notions of what "Indian art" is, or should be, than from a sense of artistic merit. Museum professionals, in particular, have a history of paying lip-service to Native American artists, of listening to their views, ideas and concerns, without ever absorbing the messages in the words. We are so dead-set on discovering and interpreting our stereotyped, preconceived visions of the so-called "traditional Indian" and "traditional Indian art" that we fail to see anything outside our predetermined mindset.

For a half millennium Native Americans have endured campaigns of subjugation, scientific investigation, freeze-dried encapsulation and misinterpretation in works of art, photographs and bigger-than-life monuments. Unwilling participants in governmental policies aimed at assimilating them into the so-called mainstream of society, they have been culturally pummeled to the point of being presumably unrecognizable even to themselves, or, more to the point, to the dominant society.

The Native American fine arts movement is an advent of the twentieth century, born out

DAVID BRADLEY (born 1954)

CHIPPEWA/LAKOTA

American Indian Gothic (1983)

Color lithograph, 26/50 ed.; Buffalo Bill Historical Center,
Gift of Mrs. Damaras D. W. Ethridge

"When I first entered the somewhat glamorous world of professional art, I thought I would steer clear of politics and keep my life as simple and positive as possible. Eventually, I realized that Indians are, by definition, political beings . . . I saw the continual exploitation of the Indian art community by museums in the Southwest . . . I witnessed multi-million dollar fraud by pseudo-Indian artists . . . and so [I] began to speak out on what I saw as widespread corruption in the art world" (Hill, *Creativity Is Our Tradition*, p. 98).

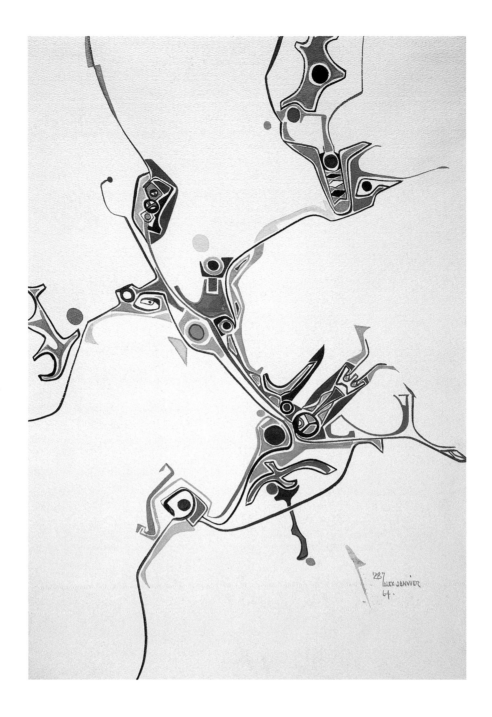

ALEX JANVIER (born 1935)

CHIPEWAY

Channelled Equality

Watercolor on paper; 15 × 22 in.

Glenbow Museum

113

of conditions "created by an officially ordained program of cultural genocide" and a strong will of survival and cultural adaptation.[2] For the better part of its existence, the Native American fine arts movement has been defined and interpreted by an ever-changing, select group of non-native "experts." In the early stages of this development, the role of Native American fine arts chronicler was commonly held by ethnologists and anthropologists. Fine art exhibitions by First Peoples generally occupied an interpretative space in which paintings and sculptures were displayed alongside pottery, basketry and beadwork.

Later, the role of chronicler was shared by art historians and other aficionados. During this phase, native fine art took on a new and special meaning. It became mystical and aesthetically pleasing to look at, but relatively few understood or appreciated the cultural and social significance of such work. native fine art was no longer an awkward extension of the "primitive" art world, yet it was not fully recognized in the same light as its non-native counterpart. Rarely, if ever, were the works of native artists included in the permanent fine arts galleries of major museums. Art history books referred to native American art only in passing and usually more in association with folk art. Lately, a number of the art critics and gallery owners have held the distinction of chronicler of Indian art and wield great power of persuasion in promoting "Indian art."[3] The combination of promoters and special art markets such as Santa Fe has created and packaged a succession of superstars, commonly non-native individuals posing as "Indian artists." Just as in the other arenas of stardom, such status is often based more on hype than on real and long lasting artistic creativity.

Today, native artists are seeking to define their own identities and roles within and without their communities. As artist Alfred Young Man contends,

Before an individual can understand and appreciate North American Indian art— practice and theory—it is advisable and even imperative to learn something about the arguments that rage around it. In particular, it is essential to become familiar with the North American Indian *native perspective*. The *native perspective* should be applied both rigidly and boldly, and made an integral part of the various critical, analytical and historical instruments that make up the lexicon of art, not just when it is convenient to do so but whenever the "edge" of the Native American art world rubs up against those of the so-called Western art world.[4]

To understand the contemporary Native American fine arts movement requires us to address racial biases and stereotypes, and to give native artists the opportunity to speak for themselves.

One major obstacle in the examination of Native American art is the persistence in defining native American art as a single entity—"Indian art." We continually place native fine art into a singular framework, as if there were only one culture, one lifestyle, one religious belief and one form of artistic expression for all native peoples. When Columbus happened upon the Americas, he encountered peoples living in culturally diverse societies with different languages, different religions and different traditions. This continent was not unlike Europe, where surface similarities masked considerable differences among the population. No one today confuses the French with the Italians, or classifies works by Francisco Goya as "traditional" European art. Yet Blackfeet and Caddo, Senica and Seminole, Navajo and Apache are commonly lumped together as the same people by the mere definition of being "Indian." We generally classify native fine art as either "traditional" or "non-traditional," an indirect way of saying it is either recognizably "Indian" or not.

Bently Spang (born 1960)

NORTHERN CHEYENNE

Culture Cache #1 (1993)

Mixed media sculpture; H 28 × W 36 × D 8 in.

Eiteljorg Museum of American Indians and Western Art

"The material I choose act as metaphor for the two worlds I am from, and so illustrate how they are inseparably bound together in me. There exists an inherent tension between man-made and natural materials, modern versus indigenous—one always wants to consume the other. The trick is to strike a balance between the two, a harmony. The cocoon figure in my work represents transition, change—that search for harmony in my life" (*New Art of the West*, p. 54).

ALLAN HOUSER (1915–1994)

CHIRICAHUA APACHE

Sounds of the Night (1980)

Bronze, 6/10 ed.; H 18 × W 24 × D 14½ in.
Eiteljorg Museum of American Indians and Western Art,
Gift of Harrison Eiteljorg

"I put everything that I have into all that I do, and if it's not right,
then you won't see it on the market. I use all that I know, for I feel
that I must progress, I must not stay in one place . . . Being around
my Indian friends makes the difference in my life and in my art. I tell
my students, 'Be an Indian but allow something for creativity too'"
(Highwater, *The Sweet Grass Lives On,* p. 110).

GREY COHOE (1944–1991)

NAVAJO

Yei Bi Chei Dancers (date unknown)

Etching; 14½ × 11¾ in.

National Cowboy Hall of Fame and Western Heritage Center,

Arthur and Shifra Silberman Collection (96.27.362)

117

Western movies, art, history and literature help reinforce the notion of a single, unified portrait of First Peoples. Without the beautiful, swaying feathered bonnets and the graceful motions of their horses, we can hardly spot our "Lords of the Plains" on the crowded streets of Hollywood or Madison Avenue. Even the recent rash of supposedly politically correct, historical documentaries dealing with Native Americans has done little to dispel the Plains warrior typecasting. We see the same pictures of the same Lakota leaders fighting against the same unjust government, leaving us to believe that the story of the Lakotas, those noble nomads of the Plains, is the universal story for all Indian people. Why do we so rarely show the images and tell the stories of any one of the other 500 recognized tribes? Does hoeing crops or hunting caribou on foot create a less majestic image of our collective, mythical history than hot-rodding around the Plains on stolen horses, shooting buffalo and the occasional white settler with bows and arrows?

The stereotypical image we have created emanates from the pages of the elegant photographic works proclaiming to have captured the essence of Native Americans. This rendering of the so-called traditional way of life in turn creates the ubiquitous Indian, what Paul Chaat Smith cogently terms "the coffee-table book tribe."[5] It is the same portrait of the same "Indian," "Indian tradition" and "Indian lifeway" repeated *ad infinitum, ad nauseam*, reinforcing the imaginary depiction we hold as truth and impeding our ability to see anything else.

Such was the fate of the artist Oscar Howe, who found his works rejected from the 1958 Philbrook Museum annual Indian Artists exhibition because they were not "traditional Indian painting." Howe's reply underscores the struggle of many native artists:

Whoever said that my paintings are not in the traditional Indian style has poor knowledge of Indian art . . .There is much more to Indian art, than pretty, stylized pictures. There was also power and strength and individualism (emotional and intellectual insight) in the old Indian paintings. Every bit in my paintings is a true studied fact of Indian painting. Are we to be held back forever with one phase of Indian painting, dictated to as the Indian always has been, put on reservations and treated like a child, and only the White Man knows what is best for him? Now, even in art, "you little child do what we think is best for you, nothing different . . ." I have tried to keep the fine ways and culture of my forefathers alive. But one could easily turn to become a social protest painter. I only hope the Art World will not be one more contributor to holding us in chains.[6]

The essential question Oscar Howe asked in 1958 is still relevant—it is not a matter of defining Native American art, but of who is defining it and why.

The works of the Fort Marion ledger artists and The Kiowa Five, of Ernest Spybuck, Julian Martinez, and other early artists that have become the standards of our imposed "traditional" style were, in reality, contemporary artistic expressions when they were created. They did not follow strict artistic guidelines spelled out in some tribal manual for "traditional Indian fine art." Nor did they reflect a singular traditional style of art. Rather, they expressed and represented a particular time and milieu, the same combinations of experiences and activities that many native artists describe in their own artwork.

It is equally misleading to think that Native American art was, is, or should be static: one style of expression through all time. Native traditions, which include artistic expression, underwent a continuum of change long before the arrival of Europeans and will continue to do so. Native American art, just like American or Canadian art, is not confined to any single style, technique or medium. Each native artist brings the diversity of his or her cultural

KAY WALKINGSTICK (born 1935)

CHEROKEE/WINNEBAGO

Ourselves/Our Land (1991)

Diptych, copper, wax, wood, acrylic, and oil on canvas; 22 × 44 in.
Eiteljorg Museum of American Indians and Western Art,
Gift of Zonta Club of Indianapolis

"My present works are two-panel paintings in which the two parts
relate in a non-formal manner. One is not an abstraction of the
other; one is an extension of the other. I use landscape as the context
but any part of the natural world would be appropriate . . . One side
of the painting represents immediate visual memory; the other
archetypal memory. And both could be said to be a stand-in for the
human body and soul" (*Native Streams*, p. 40).

119

DAN LOMAHAFTEWA (born 1951)

HOPI/CHOCTAW

Spring Arrival (1994)

Collagraph; 40 × 32 in.

Eiteljorg Museum of American Indians and Western Art

"As with most of my work, I use my ethnic background (Hopi and Choctaw tribes) as a basic foundation for the translation and creation of my images. I also use all of my life experiences and formal training as additional sources when expressing my individual aesthetic vision.

"The Hopi, who live in Arizona, are a ceremoniously spiritual people. As do many tribes, they have spirit beings acting as intermediaries between ourselves and The Creator—beings that are an integral part of Hopi life. These mostly benevolent spirit beings are called katcinum, or . . . 'Kachina'" (*New Art of the West*, p. 42).

WAYNE EAGLEBOY

ONONDAGA

American Flag (1971)

Acrylic and barbed wire on buffalo hide

Autry Museum of Western Heritage

"I am a half-breed, and perhaps because of this my art is not strictly traditional. I try to paint about both cultures, the Indian and the non-Indian, and how they collide. I use traditional forms in a contemporary manner. I hope my paintings speak and tell the non-Indian what he has done to our people and also show him the beauty of our ways" (Oxendine, "23 Contemporary Indian Artists," p. 61).

121

Oscar Howe (1915–1983)

YANKTON

Sundance (1973)

Casein on paper; 30 × 40 in.; The Heard Museum

"One criterion for my painting is to present the cultural life and
activities of the Sioux Indians; dance, ceremonies, legends, lore,
arts . . . It is my greatest hope that my paintings may serve to bring
the best things of Indian culture into the modern way of life"
(*Contemporary Sioux Painting*, p. 48).

122

background melded with his or her individual life experiences. As artist Jaune Quick-to-See Smith points out, "The journey of my work follows the journey of my life as I move through public art projects, collaborations, printmaking, traveling and tribal activities. The research and activities become the reinforcement for my work."[7] For artist and art professor Truman Lowe, "Indian artists create and use material to convey thoughts about themselves and their people . . . contemporary Indian artists combine their own life experiences of their community to fuel notions of what tradition really is."[8] The late artist T. C. Cannon argued that contemporary Native American art should be viewed within the broader context of modern society:

Everyone, in their own way, seeks fulfillment and satisfaction in things that they do. I am just like you and countless millions—threading the needles that patch our individual universes into our totally selfish puzzles. We all work on different levels and though they be acute or obtuse from others, it is at the least a level on which to work. I, myself, work on many levels and each is built to give feedback.[9]

Many contemporary native artists like Leonard Riddles, Rance Hood and others consider themselves as traditionalist, but their use of the term is much different. "We try to stylize our art by outlining the whole subject—each individual object—to indicate, symbolize, or depict the old style we learned from the canyon walls of the Southwest or the hides and skins of the northern tribes . . . What makes it valuable is it depicts a race of people. You have to become knowledgeable about what you're painting," the late Doc Tate Nevaquaya pointed out.[10] Unfortunately for many non-natives, the term "traditionalist" takes on a more generalized and often maudlin context, meaning "the quintessence of all things native and Indian . . . [an] 'endangered' art form, which echoes the lifeways of native America."[11] It is the hunt for "that more elusive subject, the traditional Indian way of life," that the seemingly insignificant word commonly implies.[12]

There are more than "500 culturally-diverse tribes . . . now recognized in the United States; in addition, several hundred unrecognized tribes. If there cannot be a single definition of Indian, there cannot be a single definition for native art." Native Americans, artists and non-artists alike, "recognize that their cultural traditions have changed and that change itself is a part of survival. One constancy of tradition is change."[13]

In America, tradition is more closely associated with sports and athletics than with cultural identities. Our society commonly misconstrues fads and fashions for culture. Unfortunately, a major part of the patronage for native art does the same. Native American art is trendy. It is more commonly bought and exhibited as a fashion statement, vacation souvenir or an alleviation of a guilty conscience than as recognition of artistic merit. Art "in this country has come to mean art without culture. If you are producing artwork and are known as an Indian, then you are automatically no longer a candidate for inclusion in the fine art world."[14]

Conversely, Native Americans have not been unknowing bystanders in the fray of cultural misunderstanding and stereotyping. Those who seek to be recognized primarily as native artists or as artists who happen to be native create a particular dilemma—whether to include them in one type of art exhibition and not another, whether to explain the cultural significance or the artistic implications of an image. One also hears from the native art community the occasional statement that the word "art" does not exist in Native American

Gᴇʀᴀʟᴅ Tᴀɪʟғᴇᴀᴛʜᴇʀs (1925–1975)

ʙʟᴏᴏᴅ

Blood Camp (1956)

Oil on canvas; 38.1 × 52.7 cm.; Glenbow Museum

JAUNE QUICK-TO-SEE SMITH (born 1940)
SALISH/CREE/SHOSHONI
Untitled, Camus series (1980)
Serigraph; 30 × 22 in.
National Cowboy Hall of Fame and Western Heritage Center,
Arthur and Shifra Silberman Collection (96.27.863)

"The journey of my work follows the journey of my life as I move
through public art projects, collaborations, printmaking, traveling
and tribal activities. The research and activities become the
reinforcement for my work. Ideas will materialize or emerge in a
concrete form based on interaction between abstract conception and
tangible labor" (*Parameters*).

125

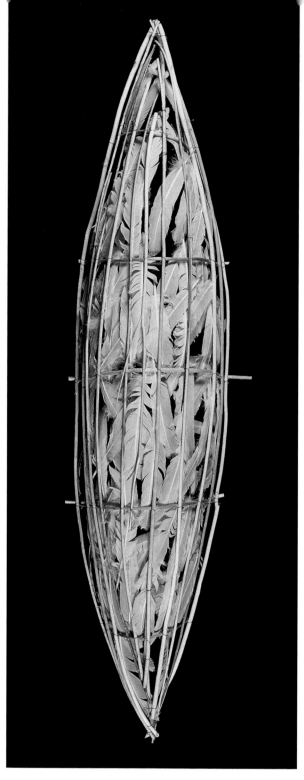

TRUMAN LOWE (born 1944)

WINNEBAGO

Feather Canoe (1993)

Wood and feathers; H 18 × W 72 × D 12 in.

Eiteljorg Museum of American Indians and Western Art, Gift in
memory of Martin and Mabel Lowe, Milton and Carolyn Knabe

"Once when I stood by the Wisconsin River watching its movement,
watching people pass by, I suddenly realized why I love being in a
canoe. First, its marvelous architecture is wonderful to be within.
More important, I understood that canoeing gave me the feeling of
being on the earth while being suspended above it" (Complo, *Haga:*
Third Son, p. 22).

T.C. Cannon (1946–1978)
caddo/kiowa/choctaw
Collector #2 (1970)
Acrylic on canvas; 46 × 50 in.
Eiteljorg Museum of American Indians and Western Art,
Gift of Harrison Eiteljorg

"The beauty of living a solitary existence is that you never have
anyone to blame. The disciplinc of the late afternoon studio and
early morning writing table are my only points of reference for days
on end. My interpretations of what I see, hear and dream require
small rooms devoid of mortal voice, whether heroic or absurd!"
(Wallo and Pickard, *T. C. Cannon, Native American, A New View
of the West*, p. 25).

Jean LaMarr (born 1945)
PITT RIVER/PAIUTE
Some Kind of Buckaroo (1990)
Serigraph; 24 × 36 in.
National Cowboy Hall of Fame and Western Heritage Center,
Arthur and Shifra Silberman Collection (96.27.508)

"I feel like my work needs some kind of artistic intelligence . . .
recognizing what has happened to Indian people . . . what's
happening in current events . . . I feel like my work communicates
to the non-Indian world . . . [and] is specifically oriented to
communicate to non-Indian people . . . It's a kind of non-verbal
communication . . . I try to use symbolism . . . I feel that might
represent something that other people might recognize" (Hill,
Creativity Is Our Tradition, p. 162).

vocabularies. While certainly true, it adds a certain amount of credence to two existing platitudes—first, that Native Americans are relics of the past, and second, that the existence of the "singular Indian" is valid social thought. To simply state that a word does not exist oversimplifies the complex cultural diversity that exists among native people. It is analogous to saying we can change and adapt culturally but not linguistically, and when taken out of context, it provides additional dry ice to our freeze-dried, stereotyped image.

There is considerable debate and an myriad of questions from within and without the Native American fine arts movement. native artist Alfred Young Man raised several issues in his essay for the exhibition *Indigena*: "Who finally decides when an Indian is something other than an Indian? How do you establish 'a clear distinction between Native American fine art, folk art, and art and crafts?'"[15] John Anson Warner, in his essay "The Indian in Native American Art: A Sociological View," also asks a number of relevant questions concerning the Native American fine arts movement. Perhaps the most important is, "Does Indian art benefit or suffer from its special status in the art marketplace?"[16]

Where does one go from here? A good starting point might be the establishment of a forum in which native people have the opportunity to tell their own history, explain their own cultural identities and develop their own definitions of art through time—the essence of Alfred Young Man's "Native perspective." There is a real need for open dialogue in which the native artist and the art "expert," the interested patron and the tribal leader, can discuss the questions and issues raised by native art.

The work of many of the contemporary native artists addresses an array of issues and concerns facing native people. Coming to terms with the stereotypes, paternalistic attitudes and racial biases that create the "us and them" dichotomy will not be easy, nor will developing an effective dialogue that will take us into the next century. It is clear that Native American art offers much enrichment to all people, and that Native American artists have much to teach us. The question remains, how long will it take us to learn, to look and to listen?[17]

Francis Yellow (born 1954)

LAKOTA

Tatanka Wan "A Buffalo Bull" (1993)

*Bronze, 3/55 ed.; H 12 × W 18 × D 3 in.; Eiteljorg Museum
of American Indians and Western Art, Gift of the Eiteljorg Circle*

"Our Elders teach us that there is a model of the universe inside
ourselves . . .We are descendants of the Pte Oyate—'Buffalo People.'
We are also descended from the Ikce Wicasa—'Common Man.'
The Lakota Oyate—'Friendly People'—are the latest evolvement,
according to our origin stories. I speak in plural because I am of my
people, I am not disconnected from them nor do I wish to be. My
identity evolves from the Buffalo People, from the Common Man,
and from the Friendly People" (*New Art of the West,* p. 58).

BENJAMIN BUFFALO (1948–1994)
CHEYENNE
Cheyenne in the Moon
Lithograph; 11¾ × 11½ in.
National Cowboy Hall of Fame and Western Heritage Center,
Arthur and Shifra Silberman Collection, (96.27.308)

"I wanted to get away from the traditional, two-dimensional type of
work. I'm trying to express the realism of our American Indians by
photographic exactness" (Lester, *Biographical Directory of Native
American Painters*, p. 87).

WA WA CHAW (1888–1972)

LUISEÑO

Untitled drawing (date unknown)

Ink on paper; 16 × 11 in.; National Cowboy Hall of Fame and Western
Heritage Center, Arthur and Shifra Silberman Collection (96.27.362)

"Tolerance: I found if I listen to the others first and hear what they
had for an *Opinion* I would receive the evidence to help Me carry on
with the help of Courage to Overlook the ignorance they express.
With this in Mind I have overcome many pitfalls in Human
relationship" (Steiner, ed., *Spirit Woman*, p. 20).

1. Aperture, *Strong Heart: Native American Visions and Voices* (New York: Aperture Foundation, 1996), p. 9.

2. Margaret Archuleta and Rennard Strickland, *Shared Visions: Native American Painters and Sculptors in the Twentieth Century* (Phoenix, AZ: Heard Museum, 1991), p. 7.

3. Edwin Wade, ed., *The Art of the North American Indian: Native Traditions in Evolution* (New York: Hudson Hills Press, 1986), p. 202.

4. Gerald McMaster and Lee-Ann Martin., eds., *Indigena: Contemporary Native Perspectives* (Vancouver/Toronto: Douglas & McIntyre, 1992), p. 81.

5. Aperture, *Strong Heart: Native American Visions and Voices*, pp. 20, 7.

6. Frederick J. Dockstader, ed., *Oscar Howe: A Retrospective Exhibition and Catalogue Raisonné* (Vermillion: University Art Gallery, the University of South Dakota; Mitchell, SD: Oscar Howe Art Center; Tulsa, OK: Thomas Gilcrease Museum Association, 1982), p. 19.

7. Trinkett Clark, interview with Jaune Quick-to-See Smith for *Parameters* exhibition, The Chrysler Museum, Norfolk, Virginia, 1993.

8. Rick Hill, ed., *Creativity Is Our Tradition: Three Decades of Contemporary Indian Art at the Institute of American Indian Arts* (Santa Fe, NM: Institute of American Indian and Alaska Native Culture and Arts Development, 1992), p. 12.

9. Joan Frederick, *T. C. Cannon: He Stood in the Sun* (Flagstaff, AZ: Northland Publishing Company, 1995), p. vii.

10. Joan Frederick, "Traditional Painting in Oklahoma," *Native Peoples*, Summer 1995, p. 49.

11. *Ibid.*, p. 47.

12. Aperture, *Strong Heart*, p. 20.

13. *native Streams: Contemporary Native American Art* (Chicago: Jan Cicero Gallery; Terre Haute: Turman Art Gallery, Indiana State University, 1996), p. 4.

14. Hill, *Creativity Is Our Tradition*, p. 156.

15. McMaster and Martin, eds., *Indigena*, p. 82.

16. Wade, ed., *The Art of the North American Indian*, p. 202.

17. In addition to the works cited above, see the following: Jennifer Complo, *Haga: Third Son* (Indianapolis: Eiteljorg Museum of American Indians and Western Art, 1994); *Contemporary Sioux Painting* (Rapid City, SD: Indian Arts and Crafts Board of the U.S. Dept. of the Interior, 1970); Jamake Highwater, *The Sweet Grass Lives On: Fifty Contemporary North American Indian Artists* (New York: Lippincott & Crowell, 1980); Patrick D. Lester, *The Biographical Directory of Native American Painters* (Tulsa, OK: Sir Publications, 1995, distributed by the University of Oklahoma Press); Lloyd E. Oxendine, "23 Contemporary Indian Artists," *Art in America*, July–August 1972, p. 61; *Parameters* (Norfolk, VA: Chrysler Museum, 1993); Stan Steiner, ed., *Spirit Woman: The Diaries and Paintings of Bonita Wa Wa Calachaw Nunez* (New York: Harper & Row, 1980); William Wallo and John Pickard, *T. C. Cannon, Native American: A New View of the West* (Oklahoma City and Indianapolis: The National Cowboy Hall of Fame and Western Heritage Center and the Eiteljorg Museum of American Indians and Western Art, 1990).

Acknowledgments

$\mathcal{T}$HIS CATALOGUE AND THE ACCOMPANYING EXHIBITION ARE THE RESULT of the contributions of many individuals and organizations. The process began in 1990 with a planning meeting, at which consultants Tom Chavez, Carol Clark, Brian Dippie and James Nason encouraged the group to address important issues in the exhibition.

At the Eiteljorg Museum, Designer Larry Samuels was an integral part of the exhibition process, helping to shape the exhibition through the ideas he presented. At the Autry Museum of Western Heritage, Cynthia Harnish has marshalled the educational elements of the exhibition, keeping needs and interests of the audiences in the forefront of exhibition planning. Suzanne G. Fox has overseen the publication, bringing together work from all the participating members of the organizations. Carolyn Pool, project manager during the first phase of the organization, effectively organized the exhibition team in the initial stages. Vicki Cummings came on as project manager for the second phase and efficiently brought many aspects together to make the project complete. Susan DeRenne Coerr prepared the index.

Dave Warren and Jeanine Pease Pretty On Top were consultants whose ideas helped to focus the direction of the exhibition in many valuable and constructive ways. Many other persons participated and helped during the planning process. They include Michael Duty, the late Philip Thompson, John Vanausdall, Arnold Jolles, Robert Tucker, Joyce Helvie, and the American Indian Advisory Board at the Eiteljorg Museum; Ken Townsend, Don Reeves, Richard Rattenbury, Ann Wheeler, Bobby Weaver and Ed Muno at the National Cowboy Hall of Fame; the late Fred Myers, Joan Troccoli, J. Brooks Joyner, Dan Swan, Kevin Smith and Anne Morand at the Gilcrease Museum; Joanne Hale, Melissa Richardson Banks, Noelle Toal, Kim Milliken, Thomas Thomas, Jim Omahen, Mary Ellen Hennessey Nottage, Carl Cornils, Mary Ann Ruelas, Jenny Monroe, Patricia Harvey, Carol Schreider and Michael Horse at the Autry Museum of Western Heritage; John Lewis Orendorff, Director, American Indian Education Commission, Los Angeles Unified School District; Peter H. Hassrick, B. Byron Price, Wally Reber, Lucille Warters, Joanne Patterson, Betty Kercher, Sharon Schroeder, Rebecca West, Gina Schneider, Sarah Laughlin, Elizabeth Holmes and the Plains

134

Indian Museum Advisory Board at the Buffalo Bill Historical Center. Michael T. Bies, archaeologist with the Bureau of Land Management in Worland, Wyoming, also assisted.

Guadalupe Tafoya at the Millicent Rogers Museum provided support in the early stages. Thanks are also due at the Heard Museum to Martin Sullivan, Margaret Archuleta and Gina Laczko; to Stuart A. Chase, Kent Ahrens and Robyn Peterson at the Rockwell Museum; to Robert Janes and Patricia Ainslie at the Glenbow Museum; Dan Provo, William Kerr, and Jane Lavino at the National Museum of Wildlife Art; and Rick Stewart at the Amon Carter Museum.

The exhibition and its national tour were made possible by Ford Motor Company. Additional funding has been provided by the National Endowment for the Humanities, a federal agency, and The Rockefeller Foundation.

Publication of this catalogue has been supported in part by the National Endowment for the Arts, a federal agency.

About the Contributors

PETER H. HASSRICK is founding director of The Georgia O'Keefe Museum in Santa Fe, New Mexico. He previously served as Director of the Buffalo Bill Historical Center, Cody, Wyoming, for 20 years. He served as Chairman of the Board of Museums West while *Powerful Images: Portrayals of Native America* was being developed.

DAVE WARREN is a member of the Santa Clara (Tewa) tribe. In 1993, he retired from the Smithsonian Institution, where he was Special Assistant for Applied Community Research, Office of the Assistant Secretary for Public Service, and founding Deputy Director, National Museum of the American Indian.

SARAH E. BOEHME is the John S. Bugas Curator of the Whitney Gallery of Western Art, Buffalo Bill Historical Center, Cody, Wyoming. She earned her Ph.D. in art history from Bryn Mawr College in 1994. She has published extensively on Western American art. Most recently, she co-authored *Seth Eastman: A Portfolio of North American Indians*, published in 1995.

EMMA I. HANSEN is Curator of the Plains Indian Museum, Buffalo Bill Historical Center, Cody, Wyoming. A cultural anthropologist who studied at the University of Oklahoma, she is a specialist in Plains Indian cultures. She has taught anthropology and sociology at Oklahoma University, has served as a visiting scholar and curator at Dartmouth College, and has worked with Indian tribes in Oklahoma and the northern Plains developing tribal programs for cultural preservation. She is an enrolled member of the Pawnee tribe of Oklahoma.

GERALD CONATY is Senior Curator of Ethnology, Glenbow Museum, Calgary, Alberta, Canada. His research interests are Blackfoot ethnohistory and museology. As an adjunct assistant professor at the University of Calgary, he teaches in the Museum Studies program and the Northern Planning and Development Studies Theme School. He has published more than 40 articles, and has also co-produced videos and a radio series about native history and cultures.

CLIFFORD CRANE BEAR is a member of the Siksika Nation. As Treaty 7 Liaison at the Glenbow Museum, Calgary, he is responsible for ensuring that native issues and concerns are recognized and understood within the museum. He was taught extensively about Siksika traditions by his grandfather.

MIKE LESLIE is Curator of Ethnology at the National Cowboy Hall of Fame, Oklahoma City, Oklahoma, where he serves as curator of the Arthur and Shifra Silberman Collection of Native American Fine Arts. He has published extensively on contemporary Native American art and culture. He has also taught art history and museum studies at the university level.

JAMES H. NOTTAGE is Vice President and Chief Curator at the Autry Museum of Western Heritage, Los Angeles, California, where he has been responsible for collections development, interpretive planning, and supervision of scholarly publications. He has developed dozens of major exhibitions, and published a score of catalogues, articles, and reviews. He has been part of the staff of the museum since its inception in 1985.

Index